Praise for
BE the BUSINESS
and Martha Heller

"Once again, Martha has captured the complexity and nuance of the role of the modern-day CIO, and woven it into an engaging, actionable resource for IT professionals."
—Linda Jojo, CIO, United Airlines

"In the new digital landscape, IT is no longer a support function for the business; it is a fundamental building block of the business. This requires CIOs and their colleagues to reconstruct the IT function top to bottom, and *Be the Business* provides a wealth of good ideas for how to do so."
—Geoffrey Moore, author of *Crossing the Chasm* and *Zone to Win*

"Technology has moved to the center of every business, and the list of critical competencies required of CIOs has taken yet another giant leap forward. Martha has drawn from her executive recruiting and journalism skills to create an authoritative profile of a high-performing CIO in the digital era."
—Puneet Bhasin, EVP, Corporate Operations, and president, WM Recycling, Waste Management

"Martha Heller is exactly right: technology really *is* the business today, and CIOs play a more crucial role than ever before in accelerating that business. With keen observations drawn directly from her vast network of successful Fortune 1000 executives, Martha brings a refreshingly practical point of view to the fast-evolving role of technology leaders in today's enterprise."
—Maryfran Johnson, editor in chief, CIO Events, IDG US Media

"Martha clearly identifies the increasing expectations of CEOs and corporate boards in regards to their CIOs. They must be business savvy product managers capable of defining and selling solutions that become the business products of the future. *Be the Business* is vital reading for CIOs of today and tomorrow!"
—Lynden Tennison, CIO, Union Pacific

"In this easy and worthy read, we are reminded that the days of any chasm between a business and the technology required to run and enhance it are long gone. The business and IT need to be one. To this veteran CIO and CTO, *Be the Business* is a refreshing and current book that must be embraced."
—Wayne Shurts, EVP and CTO, Sysco

"The new era of IT is changing traditional business models and asking more from CIOs. Martha provides a compelling guide based on tangible business trends and pragmatic advice from pioneering technology leaders. A must-read for any business leader confronted by digital disruption!"

—Kumud Kalia, CIO, Akamai Technologies

"In *Be the Business*, Martha Heller is spot-on about today's CIO. We can no longer just be order-takers. We need to bring value to the business and show them what is possible!"

—Paul Scorza, CIO, Ahold USA

"As a trusted advisor to many CIOs, and the CEOs that hire them, Martha has learned what it takes for CIOs to tear down the walls between IT and the business. *Be the Business* is an indispensable handbook—based on true stories and lessons—for every IT leader on becoming an essential business partner."

—Todd Tucker, author of *Technology Business Management: The Four Value Conversations CIOs Must Have With Their Businesses*

"CIOs have earned a pole position in the race to digital, but it goes far beyond technological advancements. As Martha Heller presents so compellingly in *Be the Business*, it's about tapping into our enterprise view to unify an ecosystem of interdependent beliefs, processes, and data to influence change."

—Stephen Little, CIO, Xerox

"Martha Heller provides practical advice from her enormous network of CIOs on how to take a leadership role in digital transformation, and increase the value technology contributes to the enterprise. *Be the Business* is an essential guide for CIOs to navigate the path forward."

—Peter High, author of *Implementing World Class IT Strategy*

"*Be the Business* is an essential re-skilling guide for smart CIOs who are prepared to shed their roles as technology quarterbacks and start becoming technology coaches."

—Mark Settle, author of *Truth from the Trenches: A Practical Guide to the Art of IT Management*

"Martha hit the nail on the head. CIOs can no longer be the sole provider of all things technological. Our role needs to become the enabler of innovation and digitization but in a secure, resilient, and well-architected ecosystem."

—Charlie Feld, founder and CEO, the Feld Group Institute

BE the
BUSINESS

BE the BUSINESS

CIOs in the New Era of IT

MARTHA HELLER

bibliomotion
inc.

First published by Bibliomotion, Inc.
39 Harvard Street
Brookline, MA 02445
Tel: 617-934-2427

www.bibliomotion.com

Printed in the United States of America

Print ISBN 978-1-62956-132-5
E-book ISBN 978-1-62956-133-2
Enhanced E-book ISBN 978-1-62956-134-9

CIP data has been applied for.

To my adoring family, the Heller/Vavers

Contents

Introduction

Remember the '70s?

The Bee Gees beckoned us onto the dance floor with "Stayin' Alive," Nixon tendered his resignation, and IT consisted of a couple of mainframes that hummed away in a company's back room. Flash forward a decade or so to when ERP and other packaged software products hit the scene. IT became a set of systems, important to some, but irrelevant to the vast majority of a company's employees and customers. With laptops, the Internet, e-commerce, and e-mail, IT really picked up in the late '90s; and when Y2K came along, CIOs made their way into the corporate consciousness.

And now suddenly, today, technology belongs to everyone. As CIO, you exist in a world where all of your customers and all of your employees use all of your technology all the time. With mobility, consumerization, social media, machine learning, and the Internet of Things (IoT), what had been a steady evolution of the IT organization's move from the sidelines to the center has become a revolution. Technology is at the heart of every business.

The challenge, of course, is that the suddenness of this revolution in technology adoption has not given CIOs the time to evolve their IT organizations into a "comfortable integration" with the rest of the company. This lack of comfortable integration has led to some strange phenomena, including:

- Shadow IT—rather than wait for IT and its insistence on security, architectural standards, and cost considerations, non-IT employees simply buy or build their own technology.

- The "everyone is a CIO" phenomenon, where most of your company's employees believe that they can do your job better than you can.

- The odd notion that CIOs should be responsible for driving adoption in areas where they cannot possibly have as much influence as the executives who are actually managing those businesses.

- And newfangled executive titles like "chief innovation officer" and "chief digital officer," which are nervous attempts by CEOs intent on navigating a world in which technology has become the business.

This begs some very big questions for CIOs:

- When technology all of a sudden belongs to everyone, what does that mean for IT?
- When technology is your company's differentiator, how does your IT operating model need to change?
- When technology is the business, how can we distribute technology leadership across and through the enterprise?
- How much more responsibility can IT take on?
- How long can the center hold?

I am sorry to disappoint you so early in this book, but I have no easy answers to these questions. I do, however, know one thing: the cloud, social media, mobility, and the Internet of Things are changing the way people work, live, travel, communicate, and think about the world. And while it will be another few decades, I would imagine, before we truly understand the social impact of all of this innovation, one thing is for certain: businesses are changing.

Businesses no longer call the shots about how, when, and where they will meet their customers. Businesses no longer present an impenetrable boundary between themselves and their partners and competitors. Businesses are not secure from a global force of agitators intent on mayhem and harm. Businesses cannot count on the long-term fidelity of their employees.

Because so much of this business transformation is driven by technology, IT can no longer exist merely as a support function that responds to requests and then delivers. When IT moves from enabling business strategy to defining business strategy, CIOs, their IT organizations, and their fellow executives must change their fundamental view of IT.

"People no longer think about technology as something separate and different," says Bruce Hoffmeister, CIO of Marriott International. "Using technology is just the way we do things. This means that CIOs are more tightly integrated with leaders from other disciplines. Our interactions are much broader and richer than they were five years ago."

To my mind, operationalizing this integration, that is, finding ways to distribute technology innovation, development, management, and adoption throughout the rest of the business is the most pressing work for the CIO.

"The most important thing we are doing here is collapsing the silos," says Eash Sundaram, EVP of innovation and CIO of JetBlue. "When we think about a program, we don't think about IT and finance and commercial operations. We think about how the program improves our customer or employee experience."[1]

John Marcante is CIO for Vanguard, the world's largest mutual fund company. With data at the center of his business, he has no choice but to be the business. "Today, my role is less about leading a service provider organization and more about using technology for top line growth, whether that's revenue or client loyalty," Marcante says. "That puts a new set of expectations on the technology organization, which grew up enabling strategy. Now, there are many more times when IT has to lead."[2]

Years ago, Marcante and his team built out a big data environment at Vanguard. "In IT, we wanted to accelerate our progress with big data, and we knew that, if we were to become a data-driven company, we had to build out the ecosystem. We did the opposite of what a service provider would do. Our attitude was 'build it, and they will come.' That's probably the fastest way for a CIO to get fired, but the investment has led to a huge number of great use cases around data analytics at Vanguard."

Neither Hoffmeister, Sundaram, nor Marcante wait to hear from the business. They are the business and are constantly seeking new ways to innovate, connect, and lead. But moving from enabling the business to *being* the business is challenging work. It means changing governance models, organizational structures, delivery methodologies, and hiring practices. It means transforming IT people from technologists to strategists, from constructing hard lines around IT to creating an environment devoid of organizational boundaries, and from clamping down on employees' attempts to develop their own technology to embracing end-user innovation. It also means driving change in the most difficult of all arenas: the mindset, the psyche, the most deeply held ways that we understand our jobs, our success, and our professional identity.

"CIOs can no longer control all things technology; they need to partner with business leaders to help them on their technology journey," says Ralph Loura, who has served as CIO at Clorox and HP's

Enterprise Group and is now CTO at skincare company Rodan + Fields. "It is no longer 'Bring me your requirements and my IT factory will deliver outcomes nine months from now.' Today's IT operating model has to be about cocreation. As CIO, you are no longer an account manager who calls on the finance department; you are part of the finance leadership team; you are creating with them. You just happen to have a set of resources in IT to draw from to get there. This is a different mental model in how CIOs engage."[3]

The emergence of data has had a tremendous impact on the mental model Loura describes. Some CIOs look to newly hired chief data officers for strategic direction while they focus IT on data-collection and reporting tools. Other CIOs take more of a leadership role.

"Data is turning the IT operating model on its head," says Mandy Edwards, former CIO of global real estate giant CBRE. "When you think 'data first,' applications just become a way of visualizing or transacting that data. This means that IT could wind up taking second chair to the people who identify the data that the company needs. In a world where data is king, CIOs need to rethink their approach to IT, or they will be left behind. CIOs should play a major role in defining the data structures for the company. They need to step up and start understanding this data phenomenon and become key drivers in it. They just can't wait to be told what to do."[4]

Like data, digital technologies present a significant shift in how CIOs and their teams perceive their roles.

"The CIO's ability to create that digital 'a-ha' that will transform your business is critical, because it will impact your customer model, revenue model, and expense base," says Victor Fetter, CIO of LPL Financial. "The role of the CIO is about delivering inspired experiences, which means thinking bigger about the beautiful things we can accomplish with technology. If we get this right, the CIO is in a pole position to change the business, and that's a far cry from the custodian role of the past. Five years ago, CIOs who hired user-experience people were leading edge. Today, all CIOs need to think about the end-to-end experience for customers. Data, digital, and consumerization are fundamentally changing the IT operating model and the DNA of a CIO."

I have spent the last twelve months asking CIOs how their roles have changed over the last five years. I have also asked them how they have upgraded their IT operating model, how they have reorganized their teams, and how they are approaching the new landscape of technology providers.

From my conversations with these generous CIOs, I have learned how IT can be structured around services, rather than technologies; how IT leaders are removing the traditional boundaries around their organizations; and how CIOs are eschewing standard IT metrics in favor of that small set of metrics that the business holds dear. While I have lovingly included all of these wonderful stories in this book, I was after something more. what I wanted to learn from all of my research was the following: What are the critical competencies of CIOs who have moved from IT as enabler of the business to IT *as* the business?

In gleaning these critical competencies, I have tried hard to stay away from terms like business acumen, relationships, communication, and change management. Why? Because those terms are so boring! We've been talking about these skills since I joined *CIO* magazine in 1999. Furthermore, show me an executive in any function who doesn't need those skills.

I truly believe that the CIO role is different. It brings together such a wide, and often contradictory, set of responsibilities that the skills a successful CIO brings to the job are different from those of other executives. A CIO's competencies are nuanced, complex, and varied, and, together, they are the organizing principle of this book.

We begin, in chapter 1, with "Step into the Digital Leadership Void," because CIOs are facing a host of new challenges caused by the rise of digital technologies. The rise of "digital" is either a threat or a boon to the CIO role. CEOs who hire chief digital officers risk having too many technology cooks in the kitchen; CIOs who dare to step into the digital breach have a key opportunity to stave off this confusion and capitalize on a leadership opportunity.

The second competency we discuss, in chapter 2, is managing the "white space," that amorphous operational layer where CIOs must create change when they are not necessarily anointed to do so. The white space is where CIOs learn to leverage their uniquely end-to-end horizontal view for real business value. Getting a whole slew of vertically oriented P&L leaders to adopt a comprehensive enterprise view isn't easy. But in this new era of IT, if the executive team is not rowing in the same direction, you might as well let the ship sink.

In chapter 3, "Dismantle the Iceberg," I defy my husband's editorial critique that "icebergs melt, they aren't dismantled" and address the legacy challenge facing every CIO, regardless of his or her company's history or industry. Your customers and employees are screaming for new capabilities, but you need to pay off that technical debt. In this chapter, we learn how CIOs are introducing the new while managing the old.

You know how your internal business partners think that IT is free? Well, read chapter 4 to learn how CIOs are turning IT consumers into coinvestors and creating a business community knowledgeable about the true costs of IT. When IT is the business, the entire company must have accountability for how we are spending those precious IT dollars.

IT enables. IT supports. IT drives from the back seat. How do we take a generation of backseat inhabitants and turn them into leaders? How do we teach CIOs who have grown up enabling business strategy to step up to the table and define it? How do we get the entire CIO profession to do the "gut check" it takes to have a point of view on *what* to do, not just *how* to do it? In chapter 5, "Lead," we hear from CIOs who do not wait to be asked.

In chapter 6, we focus on storytelling, a powerful tool in selling abstract concepts to a wide array of stakeholders who come from vastly different backgrounds and points of view. If you want to create a vision, tell a good story. Your message will go much farther as a memorable tale than as an architectural schematic.

On the lookout for that up-and-coming IT leader who is as well versed in your business's processes as in SDLC? Well, keep looking. As an executive recruiter, I am elbow deep in the talent market for your senior leaders, and my team and I kiss a lot of frogs before we find your hire. The reason: most companies still live for today and are not cultivating the blended leaders they will need tomorrow. In chapter 7, "Grow Blended Executives," we learn about the attributes that CIOs need in their teams, when IT is the business, and how they are developing that talent.

In chapter 8, we take on the book's title competency, "be the business." Here I address, among other things, that pesky but growing conundrum of shadow IT. We discuss approaches to engaging—not combatting—end users who develop or buy their own technology. We meet CIOs who are taking down the walls they have built around IT, and who are finally letting go of control and resources. We hear from CIOs who function as broad and influential enterprise leaders who happen to manage the IT function, as opposed to siloed managers focused on IT alone.

In chapter 9, we acknowledge that every company is becoming a technology company, and that where IT stops and "product" starts is beginning to blur. It is time for CIOs to stop talking about projects and applications and start bringing a product management mindset to IT. CIOs must start to "think product" regardless of whether the product is for internal use or in the direct line of revenue.

In the new era of IT, nine-month projects are a thing of the past. From Agile development to DevOps, to driving major cultural change, CIOs are finding ways to deliver products and value at a breakneck pace. In chapter 10, "Go Faster," we hear how CIOs are managing to move quickly, without sacrificing security or quality.

Being the business is not merely knowing the business, nor is it partnering with or delivering to the business. Being the business is a mindset change born of our technology revolution. It is the deep shift in perspective that helps us to spread technology leadership across the company and to acknowledge that IT belongs to everyone. Driving business process change is hard, but driving perspective change is even harder. It is my sincere desire that at least one idea in *Be the Business* makes your job a little easier. Enjoy!

Chapter 1

Step into the Digital Leadership Void

Bask Iyer, CIO of VMware, once told me about the "CEO missing-out syndrome." It goes like this:

Most CEOs really like their CIOs. "My CIO is great," they say. "She has kept costs down, has secured our enterprise, and runs a highly available infrastructure. In fact, she has done everything I have asked her to do since I hired her five years ago. However, I feel like I'm missing out. What with all of that innovation coming out of Silicon Valley," these CEOs worry, "I must be missing out on some really cool digital disrupter that my competitors have surely discovered."[1]

CEOs who suffer from the missing-out syndrome do one of three things:

• They anoint their CIO, formally or informally, as head of innovation and charge her with charting the company's digital future.

• They fire their CIO and hire a new one who arrives all shiny with the promise of digital innovation.

- They gently push their trusted CIO to the operational margins and hire a chief digital officer (CDO), someone with a background in marketing, strategy, or product development to build and drive a digital roadmap.

This last move can spell real trouble for a company, says Iyer. "I've encountered many CDOs who can talk a good game," he says. "They've read enough about digital technologies and have used enough mobile apps to convince the CEO that they are the right digital leader for the company. They come in and everyone loves them... for about six months. But they don't really understand how to deliver technology change, so they flame out. A year later, they are gone, and it is the CIO who is left picking up the pieces."

Currently, the average tenure for a CIO is five years. This means that a company can reel from major IT strategy shifts ("Outsource all of it!" "Bring it back inside!" "One turnkey solution!" "Best of breed!") twice every decade. That's a whole lot of change and a whole lot of money for an executive team to stomach. But CDOs, who arrive with their own list of technology investments, have tenures of eighteen months or so. They come in, set the strategy, and then leave before the ink is dry on their new vendor contracts. With two technology executives, each coming and going in a few short years, senior management winds up confused, frustrated, and farther away than ever from the promise of digital.

"It appears we are experiencing a revival of a tried and failed axiom that the IT needs of a large enterprise are best served by the adoption of a joint technology leader configuration," says Bob DeRodes, who has served as CIO of Home Depot and Target. "This concept is best described as having one bright, energetic technology leader charged with inventing new 'digital' capabilities while the other IT leader (the CIO) oversees 'traditional' IT. Two IT leaders means two IT strategies, two IT architectures, and one assurance of high cost and low interoperability."

What's more, chief digital officers are often really chief marketing officers (CMOs) who have boned up on digital technologies. But "digital" is so much more than marketing. "We are so digital," some CEOs think. "We no longer use print ads; we advertise on social media now!" But they are missing the point. Digital is not only a new way to market; it represents an entirely new operating model.

Dave Truzinski was named CDO a year after joining wireless provider NII Holdings as CIO. To him, a digital strategy is one that acknowledges that "algorithms trump organizations." According to Truzinksi, "For years, we've been taught that when we have a business problem, we can solve it by bringing teams together and that the more people we have, the more power we have. But that thinking is a by-product of how organizations have evolved. People and processes create latency; algorithms create speed. In the digital age, we need to move our core business processes to algorithms. Imagine what would happen if we automated everything your back office teams did and then told them, 'Now that you are free of that manual work, spend more time thinking about your customer and driving top-line revenue.'"[2]

Moving an entire organization from industrial thinking to digital thinking is a big job. We are talking about an operating model that has been with us since the nineteenth century that we are trying to change in only a handful of years. Does a marketing executive have the end-to-end process knowledge to bring digital to the back office? Can a career strategist tie a social-media strategy to the messy quagmire of your infrastructure? Does a product executive have the broad influencing skills to change the way an executive team understands every facet of their business?

I doubt it, and Bask Iyer does too. "In many instances, a company's most promising digital leader is the CIO," he says. "Digital transformation is more than painting a shiny picture of the future; digital transformation means tying the back end to the front end, which CIOs have done over and over again."

Becoming a Digital Leader

A digital-leadership void is afoot, which represents either a threat or an opportunity to the CIO. One viable option, of course, is to acknowledge the existence of your company's new CDO and develop a solid relationship with her or him. You have played this role in the past by partnering with sales, marketing, product, and the like. But, in the past, those partners have not been as involved in making technology investment decisions as the CDO is today. If your CDO is not in it for the long-haul, then picking up after this new technology leader may not be much fun.

Your other option is to see the void as an opportunity and step directly into it. Should you choose the latter path, you have work to do, especially if your CEO sees you as more operational than strategic.

Change Your Mindset

Aaron Levie, CEO of the enterprise cloud company Box, places CIOs at the center of what he calls "the industrialist's dilemma," where companies that have been around for a while rely on big teams, lots of plants, and big equipment—all of which become a legacy drag on innovation. This is true of CIOs and their infrastructure as well. "There is a tendency for CIOs to ask what assets they have and how to repurpose them for a new era," says Levie. "When really, you have to do away with your legacy environments and vendors, if you're going to be competitive in this new digital economy."[3]

Digital leaders need a digital mindset, which is about much more than social media. If you simply must own all of your IT, and you need big teams to get things done, you may not be ready for a digital leadership role.

Get Strategic

We all know about Maslow's hierarchy of needs, which points out that we tend to take care of food and shelter before worrying about socializing and self-esteem. This goes for CIOs as well, who should not waste their time proposing digital strategy if email isn't working. Being operationally efficient merely serves as table stakes. "Someone once told me that, when your operations are not good, you should not talk strategy," says Iyer. "Fair enough. But the opposite is also true. If your operations are good, then you must talk strategy. You can always cut more costs, but you need to break off from an 'efficiency' way of thinking if you are going to evolve into this new leadership mode."

Stop Serving and Start Leading

For years, we have been telling our IT teams that the business owns IT projects and that our job, as CIOs, is to support and enable. Sure, we can advise on IT investment strategy, but the business sponsor owns the outcome of those investments. If this is the message we are sending future CIOs, how can we raise a generation of IT leaders? How do we teach IT professionals to serve and to lead simultaneously? "The old story is, IT enables and supports the business, IT is in service to the business, the business owns the project and the job of IT is to deliver," says Iyer. "That's what we've been telling our IT leadership teams for an awfully long time now. But if CIOs are going to step into a digital leadership role, they need to change that thinking."

Iyer thinks back to a CIO position earlier in his career when he and his team had some ideas for innovating on a major product. "We were so focused on operations, and so worried about the political backlash from moving in on the product group's territory, that we didn't bring our ideas forward," he recalls. "In retrospect, we should have played it differently because we could have made a significant difference for our customers and our business."

Years later, Iyer is not making that same mistake. "I don't need to have a business sponsor for everything we do in IT," he says. "I always have two or three innovative projects going on in IT where I, as CIO, am the sponsor."

Ask for the Job

During the year that Dave Truzinski spent as CIO of NII Holdings, he was vocal about the notion that digital engagement with NII's customers would be the only business model to survive in the future, and he was named to the digital leadership position. "The very fact that I had been named CDO signaled to the entire company that we have to move to a new business model," says Truzinksi. "The CDO title represented the recognition that we could no longer do business in the 'industrial age' way."

For Donagh Herlihy, the move into digital started during his interview for the CIO position at Bloomin' Brands, which runs Outback Steakhouse, Carrabba's Italian Grill, and other restaurants. During his executive committee meetings, "the conversation focused on the shifting world of restaurant technology, and how companies are trying to differentiate through digital," says Herlihy, now EVP of digital and CIO at the company. "We talked about how marketing, technology, and store operations have to work together to create and deploy digital solutions to deliver a great customer experience. And while collaboration between these groups is critical, we all felt that we needed one member of the executive leadership team to be on the hook for ensuring we had a holistic strategy, roadmap, and investment plan."[4]

Get to Know Your CMO

While we can all acknowledge that digital encompasses much more than marketing, CIOs who don't have a great relationship with their CMO will not have much of a shot at the digital leadership position. "How do you know when the CIO and the CMO don't get along?" asks Jay Ferro, CIO of the American Cancer Society. "When the CEO hires a chief digital officer. The CDO role is a Band-Aid for two executives who can't get along."

This CIO/CMO relationship business is new. Fifteen years ago, marketing was not IT's focus. IT grew up with finance, supply chain, and operations, while marketing went to their agencies for technology solutions. "To build a trusted relationship with your marketing function, you need to get out with your end customers," says Herlihy. "Without knowledge of your customer, it will be hard to gain credibility with marketing, and without credibility with marketing, it will be tough to move into a digital leadership role."

Making Digital an Enterprise Capability

Your operational house is in order, you are thinking "digital," you and the CMO are best buddies, and you have stepped into the digital leadership void. Whether you have "digital" in your title or not, it is time to make digital an enterprise capability. This is not easy work. If you are like most CIOs, you see digital innovation happening all over your company. You are happy to see this activity, but you wonder how to wrangle it into a core enterprise strategy that can scale.

The Digital Center of Excellence

To Rhonda Gass, CIO of Stanley Black & Decker, the $11 billion diversified industrial company, "IT is no longer just about being the back-office provider or supporter of transactions. The world is so digital, we are now providing leadership in serving, winning, and retaining customers."

To provide that digital leadership, Gass and a business unit president have jointly created the "digital accelerator group," which identifies opportunities for digital products and processes across the entire company. "It was important that the digital accelerator group not just be led by technology alone," she says. "We needed it to be run by someone accountable for delivering products to the paying customer, which is not something IT traditionally does. We need our business leaders to stop equating digital with technology and to understand that they need to develop digital capabilities within their own businesses."

For Dave Smoley, CIO of AstraZeneca, getting the company's business leaders to focus on an enterprise-wide digital strategy is a work in progress. "The reality is, we've got pockets of digital activity all over the place," says Smoley, who has been CIO of the $26 billion pharmaceutical company since 2013. "Our commercial business is focused on social and content creation, global medicine development is working with sensors and smart devices, oncology is looking at digital injection technologies, and we have multiple groups using digital to improve the patient experience."

Smoley loves to see all of this focus on digital but, as of yet, sees only individual strategies. "Everyone is chasing the same problem, but we are not talking to each other," he says.

For Smoley, the keys to bringing all of that digital innovation together are relationships and governance. "We need partnerships with the business so that we can assist in the identification and selection of technology, anticipate scale-up opportunities, and enable a network of common interest that provides visibility to what each group is doing," he says. "We need to work with these teams to ensure that their digital activity lines up with our corporate strategy. We need policies, rules, and the ability to fail fast and learn. Our goal is not to control the innovation but to facilitate the networking that results in learning, faster success, and a core digital strategy."

As a precursor to developing a governance model to facilitate an enterprise digital strategy, Smoley led the executive team in a conversation about what AstraZeneca should be doing in digital. That conversation went well enough that Smoley took it a step further.

"I took the CEO and executive staff, and we spent a week in San Francisco," says Smoley. "My CTO and I hosted the trip. We met with a group of really interesting cloud companies, some with products and services specifically for the life sciences."

After meeting with some bigger players, Smoley and his CTO curated a half day of meetings with startup companies. "We did speed dating with a bunch of healthcare-related technology companies, and our executives were completely blown away," he says. Some of AstraZeneca's leaders thought that the trip would be a waste of time. Why should they travel so far just to meet some technology companies? "By the end of day one, their eyes were as big as saucers," Smoley says. "They couldn't believe how much innovation was in the room. They said, 'We need to be part of this, and we don't have to do it all on our own.'"

From the goodwill created on the San Francisco tour, Smoley established AstraZeneca's first "digital center of excellence." To lead the center, he enlisted a marketing leader from elsewhere in the company who had both the customer perspective and some experience with systems implementation.

"The digital center of excellence spans the whole digital strategy piece, including social, apps, websites, devices, sensors, data analytics—all of it," Smoley says. While the center is a business construct that stands next to IT, Smoley's CTO is an official member of the group. "I want to make sure we're having one conversation around what technology can and can't do, not two," Smoley says. "We want to avoid the scenario where there's the digital conversation and then there's the IT conversation."

AstraZeneca's CTO has considerable responsibility in the digital center of excellence. He scans the horizon for new technologies; connects people across the business who are looking for technology solutions with the right VCs, IT staff, or IT vendor partners; and develops policies and standards around platforms and development.

As CIO, Smoley's responsibility is to get the center off the ground, select the right leader from the business to take it from infancy to maturation, and champion "digital" as an enterprise-wide strategy.

"People have varying levels of urgency on digital," says Smoley. "Some think we have other things to think about and can wait, and others believe we'll be left behind if we don't move now. My role is to facilitate the conversation and build the digital center of excellence model so we are informed and ready to take full advantage as opportunities present themselves. Digital is an emotional area and a new space. There are no clear roadmaps."

The CIO As Digital Communicator

Taking on the role of the digital CIO involves more than bringing digital capabilities to your business. In a world whose employees and customers are becoming accustomed to blogs and YouTube and Twitter, "you have to be digital yourself," says Andrew Wilson, CIO of Accenture. "You need a leadership style that appeals to the postmillennials; you need to be good on camera."[5]

Wilson differentiates digital CIOs from traditional CIOs. The digital CIO, says Wilson, is an orchestrator of a whole new supply chain of technology providers, a consultant who brings game-changing ideas to the business, and a new kind of communicator. The digital CIO is a role model for other executives still caught in legacy thinking, legacy operations, and legacy approaches to communication. "CIOs can no longer sit there with an IT budget waiting for the business to make demands," Wilson says. "Technology is pervasive and always changing; the digital CIO should be the first to say, 'technology can do this in the business.' That is different from the past."

So, how does the CIO of a global company of more than three hundred thousand employees, many of them under the age of thirty, demonstrate digital leadership?

For Wilson, who spent more than twenty years running an Accenture business before he became CIO in 2013, digital leadership permeates everything he does, from organizational design to SDLC, to how he communicates to his organization.

"As CIO for a company that employs a large number of postmillennials, I need to cultivate a brand that makes sense to that generation," Wilson says. "So, I do not write e-mails; I produce TV shows."

CIO Live is a TV show that Wilson broadcasts quarterly to Accenture's entire IT organization. It is shot with multiple cameras, on a set, and before a studio audience. "Imagine *The Tonight Show* with guests from the business and our senior leadership team," says Wilson. "I open with a monologue that reflects on news headlines, some of the themes I am hearing from the Accenture marketing team, our critical measures of success, and key messages from our executive leadership. When we were launching an upgraded CRM solution and were about to relaunch our website, I talked about all of that."

Wilson might have a guest from the marketing team demo the new website or ask his DevOps lead to stand up, "weatherman style," to walk through a new dashboard. "The PowerPoint is dead," says Wilson. "Digital CIOs need to communicate with digital products."

Accenture is a sprawling global organization where Wilson's guests may not be able to make it to the studio. "The head of our digital practice was good enough to join me, even though he was on vacation when I wanted him to be on the show," says Wilson. "So he participated on the big screen just over my shoulder."

Wilson doesn't stop with the TV show; he is turning *CIO Live* into a social media phenomenon within Accenture. "Before the show, people start tweeting that they are on their treadmill ready for *CIO Live*, and I post photos to my blog of me in makeup," he says. "People across the company get together and watch the show as teams."

CIO Live has been such a hit that Wilson has set up a virtual TV studio and green screen at home, which will enable him to broadcast more than four times a year. "I call it *Virtual Live*, and it is linked to my blog," he says. "These are seven-minute vignettes where I interview members of the IT leadership team on topics of interest to the entire IT organization."

Conclusion

The chief digital officer role is transient. It is the byproduct of an executive team's surprise and confusion over their company's sudden transformation into a technology business. After nearly fifty years in IT, Bob DeRodes has seen the dual technology leadership movie before, in which one technology leader is charged with innovation and digital strategy and another oversees traditional IT. "The movie quickly turns into a horror picture—complete with creepy actors, disappearing bodies, gnashing of teeth, and an all-too-unceremonious public beheading of the CIO," says DeRodes.

In the new era of IT, digital does not mean handing technology leadership wholesale to a new executive nor does it mean keeping it all to yourself. CIOs in a digital economy need to find ways to distribute technology strategy and innovation throughout the enterprise. When technology is the business, CIOs have a tremendous opportunity to write a different ending to the horror show DeRodes describes. This new movie tells the story of a different operating model, one that involves a major perspective shift and partnerships between the CIO and key business leaders, as, together, they make digital an enterprise capability.

Chapter 2

Manage the White Space

When Wolfgang Richter was CIO of PricewaterhouseCoopers, he described to me a simple model. All businesses, Richter said, had three layers:

- The strategy layer—what products or services are we selling, and whom are we them selling to?
- The operating layer—what are the processes, organizational designs, compensation structures, and the like that enable us to execute on the strategy layer?
- The systems layer—how do we automate the operating layer and make it as efficient and productive as possible?

Senior executives love the strategy layer. And why not? Strategy is fun! It's fun to make declarations like, "We're one global company now! We've grown for one hundred years through acquisition, we run under the tyranny of the P&L, we've been fully organized by regions, but we're one global company now!"[1]

But the operating layer? Not so much. The operating layer is a sticky wicket. Who's going to tell those cranky P&L leaders that we're one company now and that they have to change their ways? (You know the old saying: "I love standards; just choose mine.") So, senior executives often skip that pesky operating layer and go straight to systems. "Oh, CIO," they say, "please won't you build us a global finance system, an integrated data strategy, a consolidated web presence, and a comprehensive CRM applications suite?"

This leaves the CIO in the often-untenable position of having to climb on over to that murky operating layer and, without really being anointed by anyone, create change there. (After all, master data management is political.)

"Change at the operating layer requires that executive and business unit management are completely aligned and committed to a single strategic vision, and what is required to achieve it," says Richter. "Change at the operating layer also requires significant investment, especially when migrating from current, historically developed processes and structures, to new and different operating models."

Here's the problem: in many companies, CIOs are asked to do their part, systems implementation, before change has really occurred at the operating layer—so they themselves must create this change but without overt support from key business leaders. With no one in the position of changing business processes, the CIO, by default, has to create that change. And this is important, because what do you get when you put new technology over old processes? Expensive technology and a lot of frustration.

In my previous book, *The CIO Paradox,* I called this phenomenon the "accountability vs. ownership" paradox, where CIOs are responsible for the outcomes of technology implementations but do not have the power to change business processes. But this book is less about problems (OK, it's a little bit about problems) and more about the competencies of CIOs who can overcome those pesky paradoxes.

At first, I called this particular competency "the courage to operationalize your horizontal view," but my editor very tactfully told me that she hated that phrase. ("It's so jargony!") So instead, I am going with "manage the white space," a critical ability for CIOs in the new era of IT. "Managing the white space," that is, using your uniquely enterprise view to create business process change, means *being* the business: it means going on the assumption that business process change is your mandate and actively applying your end-to-end view of the business, before you even get to a discussion about technology.

Michael Mathias, CIO of Blue Shield of California, sums up this competency well. "As CIOs, we have the luck and the curse to see the enterprise in all of its beauty and its ugliness," he says. "There really is nobody else who has this opportunity. We see the gaps, the opportunities, the history, and the future. It is our responsibility to bring that perspective to the table; we must have the courage to let everyone see when the baby is ugly."[2]

I don't know what it is, but something about the CIO role has always reminded me of Greek mythological figures.

For years, I likened the CIO role to Sisyphus. Remember him, the poor schlub? His job was to spend all day rolling a huge rock up a hill. He completed the task, went home, enjoyed a nice glass of wine, watched a riveting episode of *Game of Thrones,* went to sleep, and returned to work the next day. When he got there, guess what? The ball was back at the bottom of the hill. And so on ... for all eternity.

Lately, however, I have changed my thinking on this. I have a new Greek mythological figure in mind for the CIO: Cassandra. Cassandra made the critical relationship-building error of spitting on Apollo. As retaliation, Apollo gave Cassandra the power of prophesy, but also the curse of never being believed. (Cassandra eventually goes insane, by the way, so you all have that to look forward to.)

As CIO, you can see the enterprise end-to-end and how inefficiencies create waste, risk, and all sorts of missed opportunity. But seeing all of that waste and opportunity and creating a vision for change are two different things. And creating a vision for change and effectively communicating that vision are different things as well.

How do you get a committee of executives—who have spent the last thirty years focused on their own vertical function, their own region, or their own P&L—to look up, out, and in the same direction at your company's future? How do you overhaul your company's customer engagement process, when each business unit in a sprawling enterprise has its own long-tenured way of doing things? How do you create global standards in a company built on regional markets? How do you get powerful, opinionated, and sometimes change-resistant executives to pick up their oars and row the boat forward as a team?

"First, you need to understand the attitude that the current executive committee has toward IT," says Richter. "Do they believe that IT is a back-office function and a necessary evil? If the executive committee does not believe in the strategic importance of IT, and you don't have the credibility to change their perspective, your chances for success are very slim. In that case, you may want to look for other professional opportunities elsewhere."

Bringing in Industry Experts

But if you'd rather give it the old college try and not resign just yet, Richter has another suggestion: "You can encourage your CEO to bring in a top-level consultant, so that when the CEO describes the company's strategy, the consultant can talk about what the digital world will require to make that strategy work," Richter says. "CEOs sometimes believe consultants more than they do their own people."

When Richter was CIO of Rockwell International, he asked his CEO to bring in business process reengineering guru Michael Hammer to talk through the company's strategy and operating model.

"After that, my life was easy," says Richter. "Hammer told my CEO that he had to stop 'paving the cow path' with new technologies."

Richter has always found that, by using solid examples of other companies that value IT, he can help the executive committee see the light. "I always liked to use Dell as a case study," he says. "Dell has always focused on streamlining its logistics chain, which is how the company was able to put just-in-time logistics in place. When they did that, they enjoyed a significant cost advantage in their logistics, which no one else could match for a long time." If you can get successful business leaders, like Michael Dell, to make your case, you may move forward more quickly than on your own.

This is a strategy that Jim Fowler, CIO of GE, frequently employs. "Most business leaders don't know what's possible with technology," says Fowler. "They don't know that their processes are inefficient. My approach to educating business leaders on the art of the possible is to take them to see other companies who are doing things better than we are. My introducing them to their peers in other companies who are using technology to drive efficiency does more in one meeting than I can do in a month of discussions."[3]

The trick, of course, is to have connections to executives and other leading lights in the world of business process reengineering or customer engagement or social media, or whatever. Maybe you do, or maybe you don't. But the point is this: if you feel that you are shouting into an empty valley when attempting to educate your executive team on the importance of changing that tricky operating layer before you implement technology, then stop. Find someone else to come in and do a little shouting on your behalf.

Do we love that CEOs would rather listen to an industry executive over their own CIOs? Do we wish that, as CIOs, you'd had enough credibility to change the perspective of the executive team yourself? Sure, but, as I always say when I'm talking about CIOs, it takes a big ego to have a small ego, and humility (along with chutzpah, of course) is a critical attribute for CIOs. Bring in an expert to help change your thinking, establish and implement a strategy around that vision, show some results, and next time, you will need to do less work to be heard.

Using Business Architecture to Influence Others

Michael Mathias uses the concept of business architecture to get vertical leaders to agree on a standard set of processes.

When Mathias became CIO of Blue Shield of California, he joined a company that was running most of its processes in silos, with very little ability to leverage investments and capabilities across the enterprise. One major area ripe for change was customer service. "We wanted to change the way we engage with our customers going forward," says Mathias. "But we were running customer service differently from business to business, so we wound up with a scatter-shot approach. We needed to think through a new strategy that would give us a better path toward meeting our business goals around customer engagement."

Once the executive committee had settled on its new customer engagement strategy, Mathias took action. Rather than wait for the others to drive process change while he focused on IT, Mathias met with his CEO and raised his hand to take a major change-leadership role. With his CEO's endorsement, he then met with an array of stakeholders to make sure all of the functions and businesses were aligned with the new customer engagement approach.

"I sat down with our CEO and talked about what we needed to do to be successful and earned his support for bringing the business leaders together," says Mathias. "Then, I talked to our business leaders about what, in each area, we were doing separately, and what we needed to be doing collectively. They understood that the only way to achieve our new business goals was to have a unified vision, and a business architecture to make that vision actionable. In those early meetings, I didn't talk about technology at all."

Mathias relies heavily on the concept of business architecture to create business process change at Blue Shield of California. "We use business architecture to help the business define the 'what,'" says Mathias. "What do they want to be? What do they want to do? In IT, we tend to focus a lot on the 'how,' but not so much on the 'what.'" Mathias finds that business architecture helps him and his team drive business leaders toward a shared understanding of where to focus at the business level, before they even start to talk about IT.

"When I started the CIO job at Blue Shield of California, I wanted to develop an IT strategy, but I realized that I couldn't begin until the entire leadership team had a clear view of our business objectives," says Mathias. Once the executive committee was clear on their business goals, Mathias, his business partners, and his team spent four months developing a new business architecture, which they then presented to the board. "In the presentation, we are able to tell the board, 'Here's where the business is going in the next five years, this is what we want to achieve, here is how IT will support those objectives, and here is the portfolio of initiatives.'"

Mathias finds that a defined business architecture gives all of his business partners a clear view of the business and its capabilities. "The business architecture shows us our strengths, our gaps, and how to prioritize," says Mathias. "Before business architecture, we had a siloed approach with tremendous redundancy in projects and spend; we were getting no leverage. Now, it is much easier for us to agree on how to direct our IT spend and focus our resources in the right way."

Mathias's enterprise architecture team typically takes the lead in defining the business architecture. Within the team are several business architects who have deep knowledge of a set of business processes used in critical parts of the company. The business architects, along with applications, data, and infrastructure architects, all participate in the development of the business architecture. "By having the technical architects work alongside the business architects, we create tight linkages between our business goals and our IT strategy," says Mathias. "We are able to build our technology architecture in parallel with our business architecture; we are able to execute much more quickly this way. It all becomes part of the same picture."

Without great business architects, it is hard to build a business architecture. So, how do you identify the right people? "I look for people who can bridge technology and business," says Mathias. "They can think conceptually, abstractly, and they speak the language of the business. But I'm also looking for people who have a systems architecture background, so that they understand how systems work together. It's a tough skill-set, and because of that, we augment the team with some outside resources."

While the concept of business architect resembles that of a business relationship manager, Mathias doesn't use the term. "I personally don't care for the 'relationship manager' moniker," he says. "'Business architect' is a much more accurate description of the role: someone who architects the future vision of the business; someone who looks at where the overall enterprise is going. Business architects need to be able to think strategically, but equally as important, they need to make that strategy actionable."

If you are like most CIOs, you have some kind of business architecture function. But having the function is not enough. Are you using the function to manage the white space? It is not easy to get a team of executives who are all focused on their own results to look at an enterprise capability end-to-end and as a group. But getting senior executives to see the light is one of the CIO's most important roles. Business architecture is one way to get everyone on the same page.

Establishing a Business IT Strategy Board

Like so many CIOs, Kathy McElligott started her new job as CIO of Emerson, the $24.7 billion global manufacturing company, by blocking and tackling. "We had to bring our IT shared services up to the level of performance required by the business," says McElligott, now CIO and CTO of McKesson, the large global healthcare company. "We had to get that noise out of the way before we could start focusing on the future."[4]

While the IT organization at Emerson was working to improve its service delivery, McElligott and other Emerson leaders had identified a variety of opportunities to broaden the strategic use of information technologies across the company's businesses. To sort through these opportunities, Emerson did what it does periodically when the company transitions to a new phase—it set up a task force. The task force of McElligott, and several of the company's most senior operational and functional executives, took a hard look at IT, how it was working, how it was structured, the scope of responsibilities, and how it could engage better with other leaders in the company.

"What came out of that task force was the realization that the IT organization was structured correctly, but that we needed a mechanism at the enterprise level to coordinate our priorities with the business strategy at work across the rest of the company," McElligott says. In other words, she needed a way to manage the white space that exists between business leaders, each of whom had his or her own functional focus.

So, in February 2011, McElligott, along with two highly respected senior executives at Emerson, formed a "business IT strategy board," which included roughly twenty-five executive-level representatives for all of Emerson's major functions and lines of business.

The board would meet four times a year and hold "deep dive"

discussions on topics that included information security, using Oracle as a foundation for solution selling, and the digital customer experience. "This meeting was not about reporting out on the status of projects," says McElligott. "We spent at least an hour of the meeting doing a deep dive into a specific area. The whole idea was to initiate a lively discussion about business strategy." For its Oracle strategy session, for example, the board invited two senior executives from Oracle to join a discussion about Oracle implementation strategies and supply chain optimization.

Focusing the Board on the Future

After the first few business IT strategy board meetings, McElligott could see that IT was aligned with its business partners, and that she and her team had a solid roadmap for the next two years. But, when it came to business changes that were more than two years out, McElligott was less certain. "We were a manufacturing and technology company with an innovative engineering culture," she says. "We had sensors in most of our products, and our solutions were getting much more data and software driven. But even with the business IT strategy board in place, I wasn't sure IT was working on the right projects for where our business was headed."

As a way to get the board focused further into the future, McElligott enlisted IBM to interview a set of key executives and to lead the group in a one-time, day-and-a-half strategy workshop.

"We came out of the workshop with the realization that we have to put the customer at the center of all of our business initiatives," McElligott says. "That concept helped us to take a fresh look at our investments and projects and rethink much of what we were doing."

McElligott and the board reexamined all of their current initiatives and mapped them to the customer. "From there, we restructured and reprioritized programs that did not have a direct customer focus," she says.

For example, Emerson was in the middle of a supply chain process improvement program. "We were driving that project by starting with our manufacturing process and supplier integration," says McElligott. "We realized, that if we didn't start with the customer, their priorities, and their timelines, we wouldn't be able to fulfill our orders correctly. When you spend the time upfront to understand your customer's challenges, that knowledge drives all of your follow-on activity."

Running the Board Successfully

When your products are becoming software driven, and technology is moving to the center of your business, it should be pretty apparent to everyone that the very fundamentals of your business model are changing. With that knowledge, every senior executive should be raising his or her hand to join a committee charged with thinking through new business strategies. But if you've spent even a year in a company going through change, you know that is not typically the case. Some advice on getting a business IT strategy board off the ground:

• **Enlist key leaders.** "If I had tried to put the business IT strategy board together on my own, I would never have been successful," says McElligott. "You need a couple of the leaders on your side. It was essential that two of our most senior leaders from the office of the chief executive thought that the board would be a valuable use of their time. They bought into it and helped identify other executives."

• **Do some preselling.** Once the business IT strategy board was up and running, McElligott still spent a decent amount of time in one-on-one discussions between meetings testing thoughts and opinions on current and future strategic topics. "It's good to know where people stand individually before you get everyone together in a room," she says.

- **Avoid status reports.** Sitting around waiting for IT to confess to project deadline problems is a hard habit for executives to break. "Our first business IT strategy board meeting was structured more toward status updates and report-outs on key projects. But that wasn't the purpose of our board," says McElligott. "The purpose of the board was making sure we were working on the right things." So McElligott changed the format of the meeting. "Rather than have a series of report-outs, we structured the topics to provide some education of what was happening in the business, industry, or technology landscape, followed by what IT initiatives we felt were required for our business to be successful, and then encouraged discussion."

- **Leave your assumptions at the door.** "Sometimes you think you know what the business is thinking, but if you really listen to the dialogue, it might actually take you in a different direction," says McElligott. "A discussion on our digital customer experience helped me see that we did not have full alignment on the initiative. That prompted additional discussions with each of the business platforms and some tweaking of the scope before we moved forward."

Managing the White Space with Metrics

Mandy Edwards, former CIO of global real estate company CBRE, has a simple approach to managing the white space: metrics. "It is critical to have cross-functional ownership of the process that governs how the company invests in technology," she says. "Once you have an agreed-upon set of investments, then as CIO, you need to ensure everyone is comfortable with the metrics that will define a successful outcome."

Let's say that a set of executives agrees that a technology investment will increase the net operating income of a managed space. "We need to put that metric down on paper and have all major executives look at it every month," Edwards says. "It is crucial to get executive buy-in on that metric, and start using it the moment the investment is made."

According to Edwards, "It is pointless to have metrics without consequences." At CBRE, executives report on user-adoption and other business-benefit metrics monthly. "If we see that we are not meeting our adoption milestones, we discuss the issue at the executive level and make recommendations for how to improve performance. It could be as simple as missing something in training or being overly zealous about our deployment plan. If a cross-functional team galvanizes around those metrics on a monthly basis, we can course correct as appropriate."

Conclusion

Since the dawn of IT, CIOs have faced the challenge of creating horizontal change in a sea of vertically oriented executives. But in our new era of IT, the job of managing the white space has become much more important.

"The CIO is that one leader who can see everything that is happening within the organization," says Victor Fetter, CIO of LPL Financial. "The CIO looks at every transaction and every customer service experience that takes place on the digital platform. With that unique perspective, the CIO understands where efficiency is happening and where it is not. The position, at its most basic level, has moved from someone who just accepted the way things were, to someone who uses that visibility to create aha moments for all leaders across the organization."

When IT changes the business, CIOs must be the business. And being the business means assuming a leadership role in that tricky operating layer. "This is a stark change from the way CIOs used to operate," says Michael Mathias. "You are bringing people together who have always thought vertically and asking them to think horizontally. It will take some time, but once your business partners get into it, they will see the value."

Managing the white space means getting your company's leaders in a room and changing the nature of the conversation. It means keeping your business partners focused on major strategic topics that, like customer engagement and employee productivity, have a technology component but are not technology topics unto themselves.

In the new era of IT, meeting that challenge is the most important work you will do. Data analytics arms CIOs with tremendous insight into the true state of end-to-end business processes, and digital technologies create an imperative for leaders to rethink their business models. With better tools to see the truth, and a greater mandate to tell the truth, CIOs are beautifully positioned to move out of a "pure IT" role and become a unifying enterprise force.

Chapter 3

Dismantle the Iceberg

Imagine that your infrastructure is an iceberg.

The tip of the iceberg is probably about 10 or 20 (or even 30!) percent of your IT budget. It is gleaming in the sun, and holds within it the promise of mobility, predictive analytics, customer engagement, and all of the wonderful things that will propel your company to glory and riches. But lurking below sea level is the rest of your infrastructure. It's old (really old), insecure, inefficient, bloated, and expensive. Everyone can see the tip of the iceberg, and everyone wants a piece of it. But only you and your intrepid IT team can see below sea level; only you know how much investment it really needs.

As CIO, you are tempted to pander to the tip of the iceberg and make your business partners happy. You introduce new capabilities, you are beloved, and for a time, you move your business forward. But with every day that you ignore that heavy underbelly, it grows and it grows until it drags the iceberg under.

So, instead, you give the base of the iceberg the budget and the attention that it needs. You put an end to your company's tradition of mortgaging its technical future. You feel good inside, but you are frustrating your business partners and customers by denying them the latest of what technology has to offer. A conundrum!

Bruce Lee, who was CIO of Fannie Mae and is now head of operations and technology there, first introduced me to the iceberg metaphor when he was group CIO of NYSE Euronext. He describes the challenge this way: "In moving as quickly as possible to deliver new technology solutions to their businesses, most CIOs have not had the luxury of going back and rearchitecting in a new paradigm. When putting in a new tool to abstract data, for example, CIOs are more likely to bolt on web services than reengineer an underlying application. The solution adds layers to the overall technology portfolio, and the iceberg grows."[1]

What's more, the iceberg keeps your company's employees from developing the end-to-end process knowledge so vital to productivity and innovation. When Sheryl Bunton (now CIO of Gulfstream Aerospace) was CIO of Southwire, she saw this problem firsthand. "When you have a bunch of disparate systems, you typically have different vintages of technologies and fragmented processes," she says. "If one technology is five years old, and another is twenty-five years old, your users have to open multiple screens; they do not have a seamless process."

The challenge of disparate systems, says Bunton, extends past technology and process. Disparate systems have a direct impact on the way employees think about their jobs. "If your legacy systems require users to break down processes into little pieces, you wind up with people who cannot think holistically about problems," she says.[2]

But siloed thinkers, security problems, and increased expenses are not the worst part of the iceberg. The worst part of the iceberg is that it puts your company at competitive disadvantage. "Let's say you have an application that's ten years old and can only remain secure and compliant through add-ons," says Bruce Lee. "But your competitor has a new system that has embedded security and compliance. If your competitor's system is newer, then it is simpler, easier, and cheaper. This means that your competitive position against that other company decreases. Your company is not getting the benefit of the technology market evolution." The weight of the iceberg, in other words, threatens the very future of your company.

Some consultants call the solution to the iceberg problem "bimodal IT." Others employ the "changing the engine in the moving car" metaphor. Veteran technology leader Ralph Loura has another way of describing the challenge: "It's hard to start in the data center and find your way to the user," Loura says. "Some CIOs will think, 'I've got this platform and this tool and this application and this infrastructure; how do I use all of this to solve a problem in finance?' But when you start with scale, efficiency, and portability— the traditional province of IT—you are already a mile away from the end user. And once you are so far away, it is hard to make your way back."

But if you focus so hard on the end user that you ignore scale and efficiency, you have a very inefficient IT shop that users love, but that the CEO and the CFO do not.

"I think of it as shifting left and right," says Loura. "You shift left toward the business, working collaboratively to create something new and ignoring cost and scale. But you can only do that if you've got a function that is constantly shifting right by applying techniques to remove debt, streamline, and automate."

As my good friend Tom Murphy, CIO of the University of Pennsylvania, puts it, "legacy begins the day you put something in," so every company born in the industrial age (that is, earlier than 2010 or so) has an iceberg and knows that a critical competency of CIOs in the new era of IT is to dismantle it.

Creating Some Space

When Sheryl Bunton was CIO of Southwire, she and her team had an iceberg, a bevy of systems that was twenty-five to forty years old— so old, in fact, that Bunton could no longer find anyone to run them. Particularly problematic were the legacy technologies that were fragmenting the company's sales order-entry processes. Salespeople had to open a multiplicity of windows to enter an order, and were so frustrated by their inability to do their jobs that Bunton had to act fast. She did not have the time for a major reengineering effort to solve the underlying integration issues.

"We all agreed that the iPad is one of the most intuitive user interfaces in the history of computing," recalls Bunton. "Most people are comfortable with it right out of the box, so we decided to use it as our bridging device." So Bunton and her team developed APIs to connect a set of legacy systems and present them to users in a mobile user interface.

"Our API solution took away the issue of having an old system over here and a new one over there," says Bunton. "Our employees no longer had to open up three screens before they completed their process." The iPad application allowed an array of users, including internal and distributor salespeople, to pull up a dashboard for a customer location, quotes, orders, and contacts, and even drill down into an order to look at the individual line item. "We paid a lot of attention to the visuals," says Bunton. "We used truck icons, for example, to give a simple view of which items have been delivered and which have not.

"Doing this sort of mobile presentment allowed us to solve the immediate issue, and gave us the space to make the right prioritization decisions behind the scenes," she says.

The mobile platform solution returned inventory and other data faster than the on-premise legacy systems, and the advanced search features moved the customer service rep experience ahead by several generations—and all of this at a fraction of the cost of putting in a whole new system. This strategy helped the IT team to solve some immediate problems; it gave them some space to handle the reengineering work needed for a complete overall in the future. "The API approach allowed us to pursue a more balanced strategy for upgrading across a range of legacy environments," Bunton says.

Southwire's API solution is a Band-Aid that allowed Bunton the room to work on some of her hairier legacy problems, but she had to exercise restraint. "The iPad interface is not a replacement solution for a new front end," says Bunton. "If your sales force tells you that they cannot do their jobs, and your customers are angry, you can build an app like this and solve your immediate problem," she says. "We took most of the noise out of the sales process issue, but our application did not solve all of our problems."

Bunton cautions that targeted solutions are not a substitute for the reengineering work needed to modernize your portfolio: "In your kitchen, you have a microwave and an oven. The oven is the fully developed front-end system, and the microwave is the targeted solution. If you put all this new functionality in your microwave, you now have two ovens, but no microwave." In other words, you cannot have a collection of mobile apps instead of a working ERP.

Breaking Down the Big Application

While Ambit Energy, which provides gas and electricity to deregulated markets, was only just founded in 2006, CIO John Burke wound up with his own iceberg to dismantle. At the company's launch, he scoured the market for packaged software to run the business, but he didn't find what he was looking for, so he and his small team built their own.

When the business started to take off, growing from zero to $325 million in three years ($1 billion today), Burke saw that the company was running almost all of the business—including billing, rating, customer care, and transaction management—on one huge, monolithic system.

"We were growing and expanding into new markets and running the business on one centralized system," says Burke. "By 2009, it was painful to do deployments. The night team would start at midnight and go all night, and then the morning team would come in and repair what was wrong," he says. "It was hard to replicate a production environment in our test environment because the application was so big and complex. The process burned out the IT team and frustrated the business."[3]

Burke recognized that he had to replace the Waterfall development model his team had been using with something better. "Waterfall was such a long pole," he says. "We would define some new functionality, but by the time we deployed it, the business was no longer interested and had already moved on to the next thing."

It took a little convincing of both his development team and his business partners, but over the next eight months, Burke moved Ambit Energy to an Agile development model. In another major move, he reorganized his department to have nine dedicated software teams to align to the company's nine business units.

"At first, everyone was very excited about what, to us, was a pretty radical organizational change," Burke says. "They said, 'This is great. The business line managers can go directly to their dedicated development teams and tell them what they want.' It was very empowering to them, and they were motivated to make a lot of change."

But that excitement was short lived when the development teams realized that they had not solved the primary obstacle to driving rapid change. "The development teams were broken into business units, but we still had one large, central system, so we were still doing late-night pushes," Burke says. "We had a brief moment of excitement and empowerment, but then we realized that nothing changed. When it came to making system changes, we were in the same boat."

Taking a Page from Amazon

Around that time, Burke's senior developers and architects were all talking about Silicon Valley and how Amazon, Netflix, and Google were changing their development processes. "People were talking about an edict that Jeff Bezos gave to his development team at Amazon when they hit their own 'big application' problem," Burke says. "Bezos told them, 'You need to take your own piece of the large application and rip it out from the rest. As long as you provide APIs to the large application, you can write your own piece in any language. But your little interfaces have to always be working.'"

So, Burke held an open discussion with his development team about whether they could rip their application into smaller pieces. "There was a small minority of developers who thought it was possible, so we decided to give it a shot," he says.

Introducing DevOps

Burke and his team renamed the "software configuration" team "DevOps" in part to herald the direction change for the organization. "Software configuration" connoted a hurdle to get code into production, while "DevOps" meant automating and pushing quality code faster. "Our DevOps people were not really DevOps people when we first renamed the team," says Burke, "but we had to move their mindset from gatekeeping to facilitating. That was one of the hardest changes we had to make, to get them to see their role as facilitating rapid deployment in pushing code."

This meant that, rather than write the code themselves, the

developers now had to configure deployments that were so mathematically correct that they all could be done by scripts and automated software. "That kind of process really makes you think through all of the configurations on your system," says Burke.

Burke identified a few key architects who believed in the automated continuous delivery model and coached them to bring the vision to the rest of the team. "Through the influence of these leaders, the people who had been terrified to automate development were starting to get excited about it."

While Burke was reorganizing and appointing leadership, he still had this large application he had to split up, and the company was growing fast. "We didn't have an R&D department to figure this out while we performed our day jobs," Burke says. "We were all working on things that matter to the business, and at the same time, we had to figure out how to break one large system into nine smaller, business-aligned systems."

To break down the application, the IT team had to figure out which automation tool sets to buy and how many extra servers they would need, but to Burke, that was the easy part. In addition to changing the mindset of the team, the other real challenge was getting buy-in from the business. "It was now 2011, and while the business had gotten excited about the nine dedicated development teams, they started to lose faith when we couldn't get any deployments out the door. We had to convince our business partners to take the chance and allow us to rip apart the application."

In the end, after a two-year initiative, Burke and his team did rip apart the application and are now in automated continuous delivery heaven. "We got to the point where we were doing roughly thirty-four deployments a day and we never saw a hiccup. Our business teams have been on fire because they can come to work with a purpose; they can get things done."

Burke's experience is a testament to the fact that DevOps is more than a new approach to development and infrastructure. Like so much in the new era of IT, it involves a massive change in the way all professionals, inside of IT and out, understand their jobs. "Some people can never make the leap to DevOps," says Ralph Loura. "They can never really put their trust in a code model for infrastructure because they want somebody's eyeballs on the process. It's like being a parent. If you are constantly helicopter parenting your teenagers, they never learn that choices have consequences. It's the same with developers. If a developer makes a mistake and someone in operations catches it before the program goes into production, the developer never learns. But with DevOps, the developers are the ones who get woken up at three in the morning because their code failed." DevOps both requires and engenders a perspective shift that some developers embrace and some do not.

The Business vs. Technology-Skills Debate

I've spent hours on stage getting heckled by CIOs when I've dared to suggest that CIOs could use a few technical skills. "We are business leaders!" my ornery audiences proclaim. "We are not technologists!" For years, experts in the CIO role have been exhorting CIOs to be business people and leave the technical depth to their teams—or outsource it! (Haven't technical skills become a commodity?)

In fact, the very title of this book, *Be the Business*, underscores the business orientation of successful CIOs. But being the business does not mean abandoning your knowledge of the stack and of architecture and of how a new array of vendors does or does not fit into your portfolio. I will say it here and now: I believe that, in the new era of IT—with the bevy of new technical choices in front of us—CIOs need to have a significant and deep understanding of technology. Do they need to sit in as their company's CTO or chief architect?

Certainly not, but when it comes to dismantling the iceberg, an "architectural sensibility," at least, will come in handy.

Ralph Loura agrees: "To be a CIO today, you have to be the master of almost everything, including technology. If you take a CIO with a great business background and ask him to meet with a cloud-based vendor who is talking about columnar compression and node-based architecture, his head is spinning. On the other hand, if CIOs don't have depth in finance, they will not be effective. CIOs with no legal savvy will find themselves with unanticipated incremental costs from new vendor contracts. And the list goes on. The challenge for today's CIO is to be expert in a large number of disciplines all at once."

Tips for Dismantling the Iceberg

Your iceberg has been growing for forty years. Your approach to dismantling it poses architectural, strategic, and financial questions. Some CIOs decide not to dismantle the iceberg at all—just let it run its course. Your approach will depend on your corporate culture's appetite for change, your industry, your budget, and a whole list of other factors. But, regardless of your particular situation, the following are some concepts to keep in mind:

• **Stop protecting the iceberg.** "Some CIOs," says Bruce Lee, "are so protective of their current infrastructure, that they are their own worst enemy. Every time the CEO says, 'Let's go to the cloud,' these CIOs say, 'But the cloud isn't secure! We'll suffer from a lack of integration! We'll be captive to those cloud providers.' Rather than do the hard work of rethinking their architecture, these CIOs wind up perpetuating the problem. Protectionist CIOs have the purest of motives, but they are often responsible for the weight of the iceberg."

• **Change your criteria when selecting outsourcers.** Outsourcing, most CIOs admit, produces diminishing returns. You outsource initially to get lower labor costs. Three years later, you need another 30 percent cost reduction, but you can't squeeze anything else out of your outsourced operations. "The only way to get further cost reductions is through reengineering," says Lee. "These days, many of the major outsourcers are revisiting their engagement model and are having the tough conversations with their customers about architecture: 'Which applications do you care about? Which can you do without?'" CIOs may want to ask themselves, suggests Lee, which outsourcing partner has the skills to break down the legacy problem and help reengineer. "CIOs who are used to selecting their outsourcers based on who can run their operations the cheapest may want to change their selection criteria," he says. "They may want to start asking which outsourcers have the architecture and engineering skills to get them out of this mess."

• **Security is an opportunity.** Want to get your company invested in dismantling the iceberg? Make it a security issue! "Information security gives us some additional levers to pull in reducing legacy," says Bruce Lee. "People may be obsessed with a new customer-to-customer payment exchange, forgetting that a creaking twenty-year-old payment infrastructure has to run it, and old infrastructure can mean insecure data. The security lens properly applied is a very strong new lever in helping to dismantle the iceberg, because people understand that legacy systems create enterprise-level risk."

• **Don't expect recognition.** You and your team are accomplishing architectural feats of strength beneath the waterline, but if you are doing you jobs right, no one will notice. Expecting recognition for dismantling the iceberg is a fool's errand, says Kevin Horner, former CIO of Alcoa and CEO of Mastech, an IT staffing firm. "Do not, under any circumstances, expect applause or a raise when you have dismantled the iceberg," Horner cautions. "Since no one in the business sees the iceberg, and no one understands that the iceberg is real and it is ours, they cannot understand that what used to be under the water now behaves completely differently. Business leaders understand cost, throughput, and all of the new capabilities that run on top of the iceberg. These are the likely places for applause. Expecting recognition for what you do below the waterline is not advised. Do not fight that battle." As CIO, you sit in the big chair and can handle hard work that goes uncredited. But your team is a different story. Your team needs encouragement and rewards and the recognition that their hard work matters. Finding a way to motivate your "below the waterline" team is a critical part of dismantling the iceberg.

Making Bets on New Vendors

Gone are the days when you can say, "We're a [pick your favorite vendor] shop. Its new product line defines our technology investment plan."

"Not only has the consumerization of technology set a whole new bar for what people expect from IT," says Mandy Edwards, former CIO of CBRE, "we've also seen dramatic change in the options available for how to deliver IT services. With software and infrastructure as a service, we can no longer just talk to a few large, top-tier providers. We need to get really good at looking into the future, anticipating how technology will change, and chart our path forward with a much greater breadth of providers."

Sure, this new vendor has a cool product that seems to fulfill a major customer need. But can it scale? Great, this vendor gives us scale and stability, but will this investment box us in and limit our flexibility in the future? "I need to be sure that my investments today, both from an architectural and cost perspective, don't preclude me from taking advantage of future opportunities," says Bruce Hoffmeister, CIO of Marriott International. "I can't be in the position of saying that I haven't gotten a return on this investment yet, so I can't move to the new thing. If I am, I'll get left behind. My job is to make those tough choices and take obsolescence out of our investments."

CIOs have a complicated relationship to risk. Responsible for securing the enterprise, they have to be extremely careful about lowering the drawbridge to let new technologies cross the moat, but at the same time, they have to take all sorts of chances on new players. In the new era of IT, when the boundaries between us and them and between inside and outside are blurrier than ever, CIOs may need to alter their risk profile.

"Today, we will partner with a company that is so new or so small that we traditionally would have said, 'No way; it's too risky,'" says Dave Smoley, CIO of AstraZeneca. "The new player might not have the right product today (or even be solvent), but we believe in their vision and what they are capable of. When we look at our IT supply chain, we look at more than just the product; we look at innovative thinking, an entrepreneurial spirit, and their ability to partner."

But if you are going to increase your risk tolerance for new players, then you better improve your vendor management capabilities at the same time. "As CIO of Adobe, I built a next-generation vendor management office that did much more than deal with contract renewal," says Gerri Martin-Flickinger. "It did everything from tracking how the analyst community views our vendors to doing quarterly measurements around quality of engagement." A sophisticated VMO will help you manage your new slew of vendors, but building it takes some time, because the skills it requires are much different from the past. "This is a different breed of vendor management," says Martin-Flickinger. "It stays close to the vendors the way a venture capital firm would. Are they going through a management shake-up? Are they having security issues? Are they building an alliance with one of the big players? More than ever in IT, you can't wait to watch the next thing happen. You need to be in the middle of it."

Conclusion

Every CIO has an iceberg. For some, it is so old and so rickety that the CIOs who own it have no choice but to dismantle it now. Others know that the iceberg can float along for a while and, with subtle improvements, will melt over time. ("But what about shadow IT?" you ask. "What about business partners who add to the iceberg with their own technology investments?" We get there in a later chapter, I promise!) How you deal with the iceberg depends on a host of factors, including culture, cost, industry, and skills. But whatever approach you choose, you will be beset by a bevy of tradeoffs. As Bruce Hoffmeister puts it, "As CIOs, we need to ask which problems we want. Do I want the challenge of having a partner that is nimble but cannot give me global support? Or do I want the deep support organization that will bring me less innovation? There is no sense in looking for the perfect path. It doesn't exist."

In the new era of IT, CIOs need to focus on leadership, customers, business strategy, and teams. But as we work on those soft and squishy areas, let's not forget that, way down in the bowels of the organization, there is a lot of old technology humming away as the entire landscape changes around it. As usual, CIOs need to use their special powers to do the impossible: envision the architecture of the future and make the best possible tradeoffs today.

Chapter 4

Turn IT Consumers into Coinvestors

For the last few years, my teenage daughters thought that their clothes were free. And it's no wonder. No sooner would they submit their new J.Crew sweater requests than dutiful Mommy would go online and place an order. Like magic, the coveted sweater would appear on our doorstep a mere three days later.

How odd, I would think when I saw the contents of the package. This new sweater looks an awful lot like the sweater I just ordered a few months ago. True, this sweater's color is "twilight" while the former is "midnight," but still...

Then, I got wise. I gave my daughters a budget to manage their own clothing spend. As newly informed investors in their own wardrobe, they figured out ways to reuse last month's sweater and focus their investments on new clothing capabilities.

This rare moment of parenting success reminded me of a conversation I had a few months ago with a CIO who complained that her business partners thought IT was free. The business would have a need, tell IT all about it, and then be relatively oblivious about the true costs of the technology solutions that IT provided. What's more, after the implementation, the business partner who requested the solution would fail to look back to determine if the business outcome bang was worth the investment buck. The business's general lack of understanding of the true costs (and results) of IT, this CIO found, created major problems in performance, business impact, and IT credibility.

"I have to laugh when I hear that some users think that IT is free," says Bruce Hoffmeister, CIO of Marriott International. "I don't have that problem here. Everyone thinks IT costs too much."

While Hoffmeister and his colleagues at the $14 billion hospitality company have a mature process of managing IT investments, he understands the challenges of transparency between other disciplines and IT. "When you are building a new hotel, it's pretty easy to understand the costs," he says. "You know you have to buy a piece of land, dig a foundation, pay carpenters, plumbers, and electricians, and you can see the building going up. But then you turn around to IT and ask them to develop a new piece of code. There might be a huge team of developers working on the project overseas, but you can't see them. IT work is not nearly as tangible as a building is, so it's easier to decide that you want it to cost less."

To offset people's natural tendencies to devalue what they cannot see, the senior team at Marriott looks at projects holistically. "The need for new functionality is a conversation between the discipline leaders and the IT leaders who support that discipline," Hoffmeister says. "From that conversation will come projects, and technology costs are included along with people and any other costs. So, from an investment perspective, everyone is aware of what it will cost to deliver the project and has a voice as to whether they believe it is worth it."

According to Hoffmeister, because the discipline leaders are just as accountable for costs and outcomes as IT leaders, "our conversations about IT spend have shifted from cost to value."

Paul Bellack, VP of global IT at Magna International, Inc., a $32 billion auto parts manufacturer, agrees. "In my organization, we won't start work if the process owner doesn't commit to doing the business case," he says. "The project won't even get on the list unless Harry in a business function has agreed to build a business case and fund the investment." But at a company like Magna, which is highly decentralized and a late adopter of new technologies, getting process owners to fund IT is a challenge.

"Sometimes business cases are hard, either because the benefits are illusive or people don't understand what IT can do to create the benefits," says Bellack. "Especially in old companies, where group presidents believe that all IT does is spend money, you have to get them on board. You have to teach them the value of IT before they are willing or able to build IT into a business case. This is an uphill battle. It took me three months to convince my company to fund one small analytics workshop. They think we just want to spend money."

But in the new era of IT, when IT permeates every single aspect of a company, CIOs must rise to the challenge. They need to educate the senior leadership team, and with them, figure out how to distribute IT innovation, development, delivery, and management throughout the enterprise. And IT finance is a good place to start. When technology is the business, the IT budget cannot belong to IT alone. This is a concept that is easy to understand but hard to implement. It is very difficult to take business partners, who are used to paying a lump allocation, and convert them into investors knowledgeable about the true costs of IT. But the CIOs who can drive this change enjoy a collaborative investment community where everyone is focused on making the IT bang worth the buck.

One Company, One IT Budget

When Eric Slavinksy became CIO of Louisville Gas & Electric (LG&E), he inherited an IT organization that often worked independently from other areas of the business. Slavinsky saw that changing the company's governance structure would bring IT together with the rest of the business.

"Previously, IT would fund infrastructure, security, and support, and the lines of business would fund major application projects," says Slavinsky, now CIO of utility companies LG&E and KU, and of PPL Corporation, their parent company. "We did not have one comprehensive approach to IT investments, so we had a lot of unplanned projects." Without a consolidated plan, IT's resources and time became strained.[1]

Slavinsky knew that PPL needed one budget for IT, not two, so he started with the executive committee. "I encouraged them to see that we needed a single technology plan, a single technology group, and a single technology budget," he says. The concept was simple, but the change was not. "When people give up budget dollars, they feel like they're giving up some power," says Slavinsky. "I needed to show our business leaders they were not the only ones giving up their budget; I was too."

Once he gained executive support to consolidate budgets, he and his team developed the technology portfolio management committee (TPMC), a group of directors from across the company that meets monthly to prioritize technology investments. When business cases warrant additional funds, the TPMC appeals to the resource allocation committee, made up of VPs and officers of the company.

In establishing the TPMC, Slavinsky thought he might face some resistance and even concern that IT had too much control over its business partners' budgets. "By transferring their budgets, business leaders thought their projects wouldn't be prioritized," says Slavinsky. To offset that concern, he made sure the TPMC was well populated with business leaders, and he purposely left the process that the TPMC would follow undefined. "We decided to make the TPMC business heavy and the process ambiguous, so the group could better collaborate. We wanted to be clear that we were developing the new process together."

Within a few months, the TPMC had come up with a three-level process for prioritizing investments, and Slavinsky saw the relationship between IT and its business partners begin to strengthen. "When people presented their cases, they fielded more questions from their business partners than from IT," he says. "For the first time, people started thinking about projects that were best for the company as a whole, not necessarily for their own area."

TPMC members began to accept that the capital investment their business area originally gave to the centralized IT budget would not necessarily translate into projects solely for their group. It all depended upon how the TPMC prioritized the investment. With the improved collective company mindset, members on the team focused on which projects would have the most significant impact on the company.

The new governance structure instills confidence in employees and executives that the company is working on the right technology projects and, most importantly, has influenced the business community to be more knowledgeable about the true costs of IT.

The CIO Theory of Reciprocity

Stephen Gold, who has been CIO of CVS Health since 2012 and became EVP of business and technology operations in 2015, has been leading the $140 billion company on a journey toward a culture of investment management since he came on board. Gold knows that any CIO who wants to move from supporting the business to being the business has to change his own mindset first. His suggestion: run IT like a business.

When you are CEO of a business, you care deeply about every

dollar, where it comes from and where it's going. "Ask yourself," suggests Gold, "'If this IT organization were my own business, would I be spending my money this way? Is this how I would be managing my investments?' Your first step in running IT like a business is to stop thinking of IT investments as OPM [other people's money] and treat it as if it were your own."[2]

Once you've shifted your own mindset to running IT like a business, you have to change the mindset of your fellow executives. When Gold joined CVS Health, he and his leadership team ran a series of "IT 101" sessions for non-IT leaders, at increasing levels of detail, to explain what IT is all about. "We started with the structure of the business and the corresponding structure of IT; then we showed how the financials of IT tie back to the activities of the business," he says. "Then we moved on to the systems that support the business, the staffing, and a breakdown of our expenditures and how each area is performing."

Once you have followed Gold's lead and given your executive peers a foundational understanding of IT and its cost structure, you are ready for the final step in running IT like a business: establishing continuity of value. "When CIOs tell their CEOs and CFOs that they want to spend $100 million on new investments, they will hear, 'That's too much money. We can't afford that right now.' But that's because they are working with only half the equation," says Gold. "If those same CIOs were to say, 'Here is the $100 million investment; and for this $40 million, we'll return $75 million, and for this $60 million, we'll return $90 million,' they are telling a different story."

Gold calls this the "CIO theory of reciprocity" and gives an example: "Let's say the head of sales of your company says, 'If I had a real-time inventory management system, I could increase revenue by $500 million.' By the CIO theory of reciprocity, that means that, if IT builds a real-time inventory management system, the head of sales should commit to taking up his or her revenue forecast by $500 million. If they are not willing to do that, then the theory breaks down and everyone should question the project."

When all IT investments tie into the P&L, you are in a state of continuity of value, and IT and its business partners are true collaborators in getting the biggest bang for the IT buck.

So there you have it: a few simple steps toward IT investment nirvana. Not so fast, says Gold. "This is a major cultural and operational change, and a long journey," he says. "It takes hard work and collaboration to get to continuity of value."

Gold offers some advice on developing an IT investment management culture.

• **Establish an investment committee.** At CVS Health, IT and business leaders have formed an investment committee that meets monthly to go through a project review process for potential IT investments and their return. They look at the business case, the confidence level in the potential return, and the category of the investment (regulatory, strategic, operational). They then weigh each investment and draw a waterline to divide what does and does not fit into the current business plan.

"We stack rank the investments and draw a line at, let's say, $500 million," says Gold. "Investments that don't make the waterline are queued, and those that do, pass through for activation and execution. We then work with our finance partners to ensure that the benefits projected from each approved investment flow through to the P&L. That's continuity of value."

• **Remember the ongoing investments.** "The continuity of value program is not only for new investments but for ongoing investments as well," says Gold. "When the program is running at full maturity, the IT and business teams hold ourselves accountable for what it will cost to build, deliver and run a program year after year, and not just for the initial costs."

- **Sell the concept and incentivize.** "Find one willing partner with one viable project and then use that success to get more partners on board," suggests Gold. "If you show how continuity of value strengthens the business case and helps the project get funded, you have built an incentive to participate in the program. Then it's just wash, rinse, and repeat as you move from projects to departments to divisions to the enterprise."

Building an Investment Management Community

Joe Spagnoletti, who was CIO of Campbell Soup Company from 2008 to 2015, used the concept of investment management to change IT from an order-taking model to a "demand-driven" model.

"Several years ago, we saw mounting demand and increased operating costs, so we decided to design the organization for the work we were going to be doing and not for the work we had been doing," he says. "So, we took a position on the future of IT and designed an IT operating model that would allow us to be more adaptive, better integrated, and have higher business acumen to meet the changing flow of demand."[3]

In this new operating model, IT and its partners conceptualize IT as an investment portfolio where investors are always making trade-offs about how to balance the portfolio. "This new perspective has allowed us to shift from focusing exclusively on our IT operating costs to focusing on business outcomes. We now know which programs to put money behind and how we are impacting value."

Like Slavinsky and Gold, Spagnoletti knew that educating the business was the first step in changing senior management's mindset from consumer to investor. The executive team decided to look at four characteristics when making IT investment decisions: business outcome, operating performance, cost to serve, and risk. "We educated the executive teams and our business leaders about how to think of an IT investment more broadly," says Spagnoletti. "In their personal lives, our business partners have investment brokers, and they ask them 'how is my current portfolio doing?' before they make more investment decisions. We are bringing that view to our service owners. We show them how their current portfolio is performing, so they think, 'In a silo, this one investment looks good, but how does it look as a part of a collection?'"

By exposing Campbell's business leaders to all of the factors that go into an IT investment decision, Spagnoletti handed them more accountability for those decisions. "We transferred more decision-making authority for business services to the business owners," he says. "We began to drive decisions to where the value is realized. If the value is realized on the supply chain floor, then supply chain leaders have to own those IT investment decisions."

Spagnoletti's first challenge was to figure out which decision makers were actually involved in the investment discussion. "The right business leader is the one who needs to own the outcomes and accept the risk," he says. "That's not always the person who has the money. We had to figure out the difference between the finance owner and the risk owner."

Another challenge was in establishing the right level of transparency between IT and its business partners. "We decided to make those costs visible to the company so that people would start taking ownership of their investment decisions," says Spagnoletti. "It was important that they see the historical impact of the decisions they've made. Showing them the bill of goods for what they've invested in was eye opening to them. It was hard to get them to understand what they owned. That was a real education process. But once they had that history, they were able to redirect those investments."

When you share IT costs with your business partners, you are also sharing information about IT's performance, which means exposing your IT team to more scrutiny than they are used to. "We were not just putting the investments in the business's lap," says Spagnoletti. "We all had to take accountability for how we were managing our investments. This means that in IT, we had to remove the emotional attachment to historical choices and just look at those investments as a collection of facts. Our business partners would now have a better view as to where IT was performing well and where it needed improvement. When you open the kimono, you've got to open it all the way."

No More IT Metrics

While most of our discussion so far in this chapter has focused on changing the mindset of business executives from consumers to coinvestors, let's not forget our IT professionals, who grew up measuring uptime and network performance. "We don't use IT metrics anymore," says Eash Sundaram, CIO of JetBlue. "We measure everything in terms of how the company is performing."

One metric that is fundamental to JetBlue is cost per airline seat mile. "Every seat has a unit cost to it, and everything we do across the business, including in IT, is measured against that cost of airline seat mile," says Sundaram. "So every time you invest in a technology solution that adds cost to that airline seat mile, you need to bring in revenue or reduce cost somewhere to compensate. That's how we make investments."

Another metric that JetBlue uses is "departure zero" (D0), which measures how many planes leave zero minutes late from the gate. "Rather than say that we have three nines [99.9 percent] of uptime, we measure our network performance against D0," says Sundaram. "When everyone in IT owns that D0 metric, they become part of an entire business community that is passionate about the airline running on time."

Technology Business Management at Microsoft

Of course, if you don't know your IT costs, don't bother attempting to educate your business partners about how to manage them. For Jim DuBois, CIO of Microsoft, tracking vendor costs is pretty easy. "Tracking spend on third-party software providers or system integrators is relatively straightforward," he says. "But finding employees in the company who are doing IT work outside of IT is more complicated."[4]

DuBois and CIOs from Cisco, First American, ExxonMobil, DIRECTV, Nike, and other companies came together in 2012 to form the Technology Business Management Council (TBM) to develop a framework or lingua franca to establish and measure the totality of what a company is really spending on IT.

"TBM allows us to capture all of our spend in different towers and then assign those costs to specific investment areas," says DuBois. "We can look at all of our technology business spend and can ask better questions like, 'Where are we duplicating IT costs? What are we spending on regulatory controls? Where can we get more value for our investment at the company level?'"

Armed with real clarity around enterprise-wide IT investments (whether they are coming out of the CIO's budget or not), DuBois has been able to restructure IT from a technology-based organization to a service-offering model.

"We used to think in terms of projects and applications, and now we think in terms of service offerings," says DuBois. "Each service offering represents all of the technology investments that support an end-to-end business process, like lead generation or customer support. Conversations about IT used to be disconnected from conversations about our business. Now, we are able to talk about which investments will improve our service offerings."

Tracking IT costs across the enterprise, regardless of whether the IT organization or a business department has procured the technology, is a critical step in creating an investment management mindset in your company. But equally as important is changing the long-held order-taking culture of the IT organization itself. When IT and its business partners have a common understanding of IT costs, IT leaders can start taking a more consultative, investment management approach to their work.

"Historically, IT would do what the business wanted to do," says DuBois. "But with analytics tools, IT now sees end-to-end across the company more cleanly than most departments. We are able to say, 'I understand that you want to make this technology investment to make a process better, but this investment actually won't help, because of bottlenecks that are happening elsewhere in the company.'"

Because IT people can see so much, it is their responsibility to influence investment priorities, not just execute on priorities set by internal business partners. "We used to reward IT employees based on whether they delivered a project on time and whether the business was happy with what IT did," says DuBois. "But we found that making business partners happy did not always mean that we were doing the right thing at the company level."

DuBois no longer measures his team, for example, on the happiness of the marketing department and on whether marketing received their technology on time, but on whether IT increased the volume and the quality of sales leads. "That has been a real cultural change," he says.

With an enterprise-wide understanding of IT costs, and the service-offerings model that understanding engendered, the IT organization at Microsoft is now able to deliver faster. Along with leveraging more cloud solutions and modernizing engineering practices,

DuBois sees the shared investment management focus allowing IT to focus more on speed to market. "We used to meet with our business groups, gather requirements, write up a functional specification, get approval, have our technical teams read the document, write up technical specifications, sign off on those, and then we would go build something," says DuBois.

The protracted translation process was the result of the technical teams not understanding which business metrics they were trying to change. "With the new service-offering model, IT is directly engaged in business value and we can remove all of those translation layers," says DuBois. "We've taken time and opportunities for miscommunication out of the process."

Conclusion

When I get to my slide labeled "Turn IT Consumers into Coinvestors" during my CIO conference presentations, I take a step back from the front of the stage, because I can see the invectives coming at me from the audience. (Happily, none of you have started throwing rotten fruit, which is great, because my fashion strategy for this year's speaking season involves a lot of white.) Audience members get hot and bothered by this topic and say things like "When you hand IT investments to P&L leaders, you lose control and shadow IT gets worse!" or "The investments below the waterline are my responsibility! Why would I involve my business leaders?!"

Your impassioned points are all very well taken. There are trade-offs in every structured approach to investing those precious IT dollars. Whether you go all in, and bake every single IT cost, even infrastructure, into a P&L or whether you keep infrastructure costs in the IT budget and give your business partners accountability for new capital investments alone, the key point is this: regardless of industry, we are all working in businesses where IT no longer simply enables IT strategy; it influences and even defines it. This means that the IT budget is not IT's alone, nor does it belong solely to line of business leaders. The IT budget is the company's budget, and it is the job of the CIO to find the structures and processes that will turn that concept into a reality.

Chapter 5

Lead

When I last spoke with Scott McKay, CIO of $9 billion insurance provider Genworth Financial, he offered an analogy:

"In the boardroom, there are chairs around the table and chairs lining the walls. Every chair is occupied by an executive who is highly valued and highly compensated. But there is a clear difference between the people who sit at the table and the people who sit along the walls. The people at the table are making decisions about what the company will do. The people along the walls figure out how to deliver on those decisions. In the boardroom, there are the 'what' people and the 'how' people."[1]

Charged with operational efficiency, security, delivery, and support, CIOs have spent years focused on the "how." After all, unless you are in a high-tech company, technology has always been a "how." Technology delivers. Technology operates. Technology enables. But with advances in consumerization, big data, and mobility, technology is becoming such a disruptive force that it is time for CIOs to switch chairs.

Create a vision, have a purpose, and develop a strategy to bring the organization into the future. "Don't wait for others to dictate your strategy," says CBRE's Mandy Edwards. "That's the old service provider mentality. We used to say, 'The business needs to figure out what they want, and then we'll deliver it.' That does not work in a world where technology is the business. IT has to lead."

But before all of you second-row CIOs march right up to the table, you have some work to do.

Becoming the "What" CIO

If you are a "what" executive, you have a unique perspective on the business. "The CFO knows how the numbers need to move to create shareholder value. The head of sales knows what customers are looking for," says McKay. "What is the CIO's unique perspective?"

I know what you CIOs are thinking: "We know technology! We know APIs and Hadoop and cloud and Splunk, and how those technologies can impact the business—that is our unique contribution."

True, but technology is an enabling tool; it is critical to running your business, but it is not the totality of what you, as CIO, have to offer. CIOs, more than any other executive, have an end-to-end view of how the business works, and the tools to turn that view into insights. CIOs can see endless opportunities for improvement and change.

"The CIO has the unique opportunity to become the 'competitive capabilities champion' at the executive table," says McKay. "CIOs can take key capabilities, like processes for new product introduction or for customer fulfillment and say, 'If we want this process to differentiate us, here is what we need to do.'"

For Jim Fowler, CIO of GE, we are "moving from a world where people tell machines what to do to a world where machines tell people what to do." This massive transformation provides ample opportunity for CIOs to start defining the "what" of their company's business strategy. "Today, every plant around the world brings forecasting, inventory, and production information together in their ERP to help managers meet a demand cycle. With machine learning and artificial intelligence, we will be connecting the machines in the plant to that ERP, and our ability to determine how, when, and where to produce parts to meet a demand forecast will improve dramatically," Fowler says. "That is what makes my job as CIO so important. If I don't help people understand what happens when IT meets operational technology, we'll be sitting here five years from now less efficient than every other manufacturing company in the world."

But here's the rub: looking across silos for opportunities to improve capabilities is one thing; creating a vision for how to seize those opportunities is another. Communicating that vision effectively is harder still. But the real work, the deepest work, is in deciding to stick your neck out in the first place.

"For years, IT leaders have been taught always to have a business sponsor, and that they should spend their time aligning IT to a business strategy," says McKay. "CIOs have had it easy, because they have not had to take ownership of anything. They don't have to put forth opinions. They don't have to make tough decisions. They don't have to take personal risk. Ownership takes more personal risk than enablement."

Jim Fowler agrees that telling IT leaders that they must have a sponsor is at odds with our need to create strong leaders in IT. "When you have a functional sponsor, life is easier," Fowler says. "I'm running a project inside the company right now in supply chain, and I have a functional sponsor who understands how technology and lean process go together. In cases like this, I am willing to take the backseat and let the sponsor drive, because he has the commitment, voice, and credibility. I'll be at every meeting, and I'll sign up for everything he signs up for, but he is the public face of the project. While that model works, I do not think that IT needs to bring in a functional leader every time: If CIOs are truly business leaders, and we believe what we say about our ability to understand business processes, customers, and markets, then it's a cop-out to say that we need a functional executive to lead every project."

But how do CIOs, who are burdened with massive operational responsibility and who have learned—through their entire careers— to enable and support, shift their mindsets toward ownership and personal risk?

The first step is doing a gut check about whether to step into the "what" position. "The mode for CIOs in the past was to keep your head down, deliver what you've promised, and stay out of trouble. But that approach doesn't work anymore," says Ralph Loura. "If you want to have an impact in your company, have a point of view that sometimes challenges the status quo but do the work required to make that point of view an informed one."

Victor Fetter, CIO of LPL Financial, sees big data as a particularly important area for CIOs to assert their point of view. "If everybody spends the first half hour of every meeting arguing over which version of the truth is right, that's an incredible waste of time," Fetter says. "Our role as CIO is to use data to support the right version of truth. The CIO must be willing to lead conversations about how we can use that data to transform the business."

Recharging Your Passion to Lead

If you've spent years taking orders and fulfilling them, often to be met with disappointment, frustration, and cost concerns, you may need to recharge before you can show up as your company's competitive capabilities champion. For Tim McCabe, KPMG managing director and former CIO of Delphi Corporation, the attribute that lets most CIOs to step up to the leadership challenge is passion.

"Passion is a reason for being," says McCabe. "It is what drives your curiosity and makes you a better and more focused leader. When you care about something, you want others to share the vision, and you strive to bring as many people as possible along with you on that journey."[2]

The problem with passion, however, is that, with enough adversity, it can flicker out. "IT leaders need to think about how they recharge their passion," says McCabe, who offers three suggestions:

• **Expand your network.** "Sometimes we pick mentors who are just like us," says McCabe. "But gaining input from academia, technology experts, and leaders in different industries can provide new inspiration."

• **Get smarter.** "Read things you don't normally read," advises McCabe. "Get out of your four walls and learn from new people. Bringing alternative perspectives back to your business can bring new energy to what you do."

• **Look to your team.** "You can't instill passion in anyone else," says McCabe, "but you can bring it out. Are you providing your team with an opportunity to explore their own passion? You owe it to your team to put in models that provide some freedom to innovate."

Thinking Like a Venture Capitalist

Every day, venture capitalists take the personal (and financial) risk of betting on the success of companies over which they have little to no control. Clark Golestani, CIO of Merck, finds the venture capitalist mindset to be particularly useful as a model for the new role of the CIO. "To many CIOs, driving costs down is the end of the game," says Golestani. "But to adopt a VC perspective, the CIO needs to think like a CEO, and any great CEO is relentless about driving out costs, but investing in the business as well."[3]

But because most CEOs would rather not hear your brilliant strategies if e-mail is down, Golestani sees the road to the VC mindset as an evolution. As such, he has adapted McKinsey's "three horizons" framework for IT at the $40 billion pharmaceutical company.

In the McKinsey model, horizon one includes the core products and markets that provide the majority of a company's revenue. Horizon two covers emerging products and markets, and horizon three contains products that will drive revenue in the much longer term. CIOs, suggests Golestani, can use this model to understand their own roles.

- **Horizon one: CIO as CTO.** "In the near term, the CIO should be driving performance up and cost out," Golestani says. "In this stage, the CIO focuses on infrastructure and operations. If the first horizon isn't working, it is hard for IT to move onto anything else."

- **Horizon two: CIO as business strategist.** Once a CIO stabilizes the first horizon, he or she is now free to move to the second horizon, CIO as business strategist. "In the second horizon, the CIO functions as a business partner who is helping to grow revenue," says Golestani. "This is where a CIO develops a deep understanding of the business and drives step-level productivity by using automation or step-level revenue growth by applying IT analytics and informatics."

CIOs who have achieved the second horizon tend to appoint "junior CIOs" to work with each line of business or function. "Second-horizon CIOs have graduated to trusted advisor and consultant, and are driving digital business models into the company," says Golestani.

Some CIOs never make it to the second horizon, but those who do, and have done so for years, are ready for something more. This is where the third horizon comes in.

• **Horizon three: CIO as venture capitalist.** "In the third horizon, the CIO acts as a venture capitalist," says Golestani. "This CIO is looking out beyond thirty-six months to envision the business's future." CIOs who act as VCs spend their time considering several questions: How can we capitalize on the value that new technologies will bring to the business? How do we build a patented portfolio of IT processes and technologies that puts the company into a better position for licensing and driving future value beyond the business's core products? How do we carve out best-in-class capabilities and stand them up as new businesses? How do we drive business value on the leading edge?

Golestani has a team at Merck that focuses on the third horizon. "In the pharmaceutical industry, we produce a great deal of quantitative data, but the interpretation of that data is always in document form—internal reports and externally published material in AMA journals and *Science* and *Nature*," he says. "But, at Merck, we have developed some pretty incredible capabilities to do semantic analysis, so we have been looking at how to apply those capabilities to the protection of intellectual property."

For example, Golestani and his team have developed technologies that allows them to discover online intellectual property leakage and counterfeiting. "There are a large number of web channels that sell pharmaceuticals," says Golestani. "But which ones are selling counterfeit drugs and which aren't? We are able to mine the Internet and find out."

Merck has carved out this counterfeiting discovery capability and stood it up as an independent business (Steelgate Intelligence Systems) that serves the pharmaceutical industry and other markets that sell expensive goods. "This new company has the potential to be the leading industry provider of Internet counterfeit services," says Golestani.

Developing the Next Generation of "What" CIOs

After interviewing Scott McKay on the concept of the "what" CIO, I was troubled by a conundrum. How do we raise a generation of CIOs fearless about developing and standing by their own perspectives, when we need our IT teams to support and serve? How do we cultivate competitive capabilities champions when every IT team needs a business sponsor? How do we develop in our people the ability to toggle back and forth from the what to the how? This "lead but don't lead" or "lead from the backseat" message can be confusing to our up-and-comers.

CIOs are working hard to get through this conundrum. The best among them have a leadership development message that strikes a balance between operational and strategic attributes.

Kim Stevenson, CIO of Intel, has developed a leadership program that centers around five attributes that she believes her team needs to become effective IT leaders:

• **Breadth.** "As an IT leader, you need a very broad perspective about the market, the journey your company is on, and who your customers are," says Stevenson. "The challenge is to take that perspective and turn it into knowledge your company can act on." People lower down in the organization can lack a broad perspective on corporate strategy. "So you have to become an outstanding engine for translating your perspective into knowledge that they can use," she says. But translation to your team is not enough. "You also need to take the knowledge your team possesses and translate it back up to the CEO," says Stevenson. "If you don't develop the ability to translate perspective into actionable knowledge in all directions, you just slide along and become a coordinator, adding little value."[4]

• **Company first.** A fan of author Patrick Lencioni, Stevenson borrows from his concept of "company first" in her leadership program. "The team you are on is more important than the team you lead," she tells her senior leaders. "In every IT transformation, you make major tradeoffs between current and future functionality, and you need to let the company's needs drive your decisions around strategy, investment, and the sequencing of change. It's company first, your organization second, and you as a leader third."

Stevenson cites budget management as a classic example of when "company first" comes into play. A few years ago, she and her executive partners saw that data science as a function would add real value to Intel. But IT had a deficit of data scientists and algorithm experts, so Stevenson decided to invest in that talent and fund eighty new resources. "That meant I had to take resources away from another area," she says. "I had to say, 'You need to reduce your teams, while at the same time, we're going to hire eighty people out of the market.'" Stevenson's bet paid off: data science drove an additional $350 million in value to Intel over the next three years, a result of her prioritizing Intel over the needs of one particular team.

• **Systems thinking.** "The world is a system with patterns and engagement points, and you, as a leader, must recognize those patterns first," says Stevenson. "Identifying patterns is where we create competitive advantage."

While one could certainly look for patterns in business processes and sales data to create value, Stevenson illustrates systems thinking with a talent acquisition challenge. "At Intel, we are changing our products, and that means we need new skills, for example, radio frequency and machine learning," she says. "What universities do these people attend? Are we recruiting from the right places? Where does the talent want to live? What attracts them to that place? We are trying to figure out the patterns so that we can be successful in hiring the best talent for our future needs. We have intuitive knowledge about hiring great manufacturing people from the Midwest. But we don't necessarily have that with these newer skills. We have to uncover the patterns."

- **Change agent.** "By its nature, IT drives transformation and, as an IT leader, transformation must be a part of your DNA," says Stevenson. "Do you have a large capacity for change? Can you handle unexpected events? As CIO, you are in a constant state of transformation and must be good at leading during periods of ambiguity."

For example, several years ago, social media was gaining traction among consumers, but most corporations had not yet embraced it. "I believe IT professionals should be early adopters of new technologies and services, and, as the CIO, I needed to model the way," says Stevenson, who had had a Twitter account for a number of years but wasn't actively tweeting at the time. "I first got active and then encouraged my direct reports to get engaged on Twitter and LinkedIn," she says. This led Intel IT to evolve the company's internal social platform to better facilitate collaboration. "Intel employees now use our internal social platforms to share documents, plan, or to find and share information, which improves their productivity," Stevenson says. Intel IT also worked with the marketing group to revise the company's external social strategy, building a real-time dashboard and market sensing platform. "In one year, we went from having a minimal social presence to millions of fans on Facebook, and the Intel brand has been on the rise since that time," she says.

- **Courage.** For Stevenson, all of the other competencies lead up to this: "As CIO, you are the first to step into traffic, to stand alone during a period of change before people come on board. That takes personal courage."

Stevenson remembers when, a few years ago, she wanted her technology leaders to "broaden their aperture" in thinking about new technologies, so she pronounced to her entire organization that Intel's current IT platforms were "dead."

"Here I was in front of 350 people, and our technical experts, who know far more about technology platforms than I do, were coming up to the microphone in protest," she says. "My goal was to create enough shock to broaden their thinking, so I had to stand there alone as they threw arrows." Today, Intel runs a much more diverse portfolio of technologies, which was Stevenson's goal. "People are always reminding me that our current platforms are not actually dead, and I say, 'Yes, that wasn't the point.'"

Courage is an attribute that Rhonda Gass, CIO of Stanley Black & Decker, is also cultivating in her team. "Traditionally, in IT, we like to please. But IT is not a popularity contest; it's a reality show where we often have to deliver tough information," she says. "You have to be courageous and committed, but you also have to be intelligent. There are places to take risk and places not to take risk. As an IT leader, you need to be able to differentiate between the two. Being a CIO means having the courage not to cut corners to please a stakeholder and delivering the hard message that this is not a risk we're willing to take."

Knowing Your North Star

Jim Swanson, CIO of Monsanto, the $15 billion sustainable agriculture company, is a "what" CIO and has developed an IT organization that is focused on one goal: "To meet the world's population needs in 2050, farmers will need to be producing double their yields," Swanson says. "As part of the solution, we are using information technology to get them there. We are turning data into food."[5]

Swanson and his IT organization see predictive analytics and the Internet of Things (IoT) as the pathway to unlocking digital yield. "Our own footprint contains millions of acres that we harvest," says Swanson. "This is our learning lab. How do we produce more yield? How do we conserve more?"

Monsanto has combined more than five years of field performance data with genomic analysis to understand which combinations of the company's existing seed varieties will produce new varieties with higher yield. "We use location and weather data to test our products before they are sold to farmers," Swanson says. "We use predictive analytics to focus our efforts on the products with the highest market potential. The more we can predict an outcome, the more efficient we are at delivering the products that farmers will need."

To accelerate the rate of decision making and to streamline operations, Swanson and his team are deploying a global IoT platform that connects Monsanto's combines, planters, mobile devices, shipping scales, and barcode scanners. "When our North American corn harvester fleet was connected in real time, we gained access to the telematics, logistics, and actual harvest data for the fleet," Swanson says. "This allowed us to optimize our harvest operations and to make critical advancement decisions in a more timely manner."

Swanson takes three approaches to developing and delivering predictive analytics and IoT technologies:

• **Look inside.** First, Swanson looks to his own IT organization for new ideas. In early 2013, for example, the IT team developed a proof of concept for FieldDrive, a program that puts sensors into combines (machines that harvest grain crops) to collect real-time data on yields, soil quality, and moisture as well as imagery data on the routes that the combines were taking. With FieldDrive, that data was then streamed by satellite back to the company's big data environment. By the following fall, growers were able to use the data to make key decisions about soil topology and combine routes, all of which improved harvest quality. FieldDrive was so successful in North America that Monsanto is now deploying it in Europe, South America, and South Africa.

"We've collected more than one hundred million machine metrics, which allow us to make better decisions about quality and operations," says Swanson. "We've shaved days per harvest through this information collected from the field."

• **Look outside.** Second, Swanson looks to partnerships with companies in other industries for technologies with useful applications in agronomy. "With AT&T, we discussed the possibilities of utilizing their Cargo View product, a sensor technology that AT&T developed to help companies monitor their shipments around the world," says Swanson. "Think about a product coming off a farm and going to a manufacturing plant. Using sensor technologies, we can track that shipment, look at quality, and change routing logistics based on distance. This would allow us to prevent product quality loss, which is an important objective for us."

Monsanto's IT teams worked with their U.S. business partners in supply chain to complete a rapid proof of concept for the new capability; they tested the APIs and validated the platform compatibility. They then placed the sensors within a load of corn during harvest. The devices streamed data real time, enabling the operations teams to adjust and mitigate risk due to adverse conditions. The sensors also provided the location of the trucks, which gave Monsanto's supply chain people the ability to reposition truck traffic and pickers to optimize operations. The entire proof of concept took three weeks to execute.

• **Acquire.** Finally, Monsanto seeks out technology acquisitions that can bring in whole new capabilities. For example, Monsanto recently acquired Climate Corporation, a leading-edge analytics company that provides local weather monitoring. "One of the key decisions that a grower makes is weather," says Swanson. "By acquiring Climate, we can combine sophisticated information about weather with our understanding of hybrids and disease. This information helps farmers both increase and protect their yield."

Building a Culture of Innovation

This kind of innovation requires vision and focus on the part of IT. Swanson offers advice:

• **Know your North Star.** "Our greatest priority is unlocking digital yield for our farmers," says Swanson. "In IT, we are always asking, 'How do we turn information into food?' That is our North Star, and it gives us the freedom to think broadly. Vision should be something you never attain; you are always just driving toward it."

• **Speed up.** "With so many opportunities in big data and IoT, we have to move much more quickly," says Swanson. "Stan Dotson, our IT lead for R&D, led the charge to move us from Waterfall to Agile, Scrum, and other more iterative development approaches. That shift was game changing, and we are now delivering a new product every two weeks. We had to change the mindset around how IT shows up differently to deliver value."

• **Partner.** Some companies still suffer from the "not invented here" syndrome, where they believe that they alone must be the source of new ideas. "I am pushing on my organization to take an external lens and rewarding those activities that bring in insights from the outside," says Swanson. "There is a lot of innovation going on in the world. If we spend some time on the outside, we may learn something."

Conclusion

For several months now, I have been asking CIOs who are moving their companies from the industrial age to the digital age to tell me the one key attribute they rely on every day. Most answer the question initially with "communication," "change management," "influence," and the like. But when I ask them to dig deeper into the essential attribute that drives those behaviors, a number of my CIO friends say, "courage."

No one can accuse "traditional" CIOs of not being courageous. It takes courage to bet your company's future on a suite of technology products. It takes courage to commit to a cost reduction when you have little control over the vendor market. It takes courage to tell your board of directors that the enterprise is secure. But stepping into the role of competitive capabilities champion—moving from managing the "how" to defining the "what"—involves a greater level of personal risk than any of those activities, and it requires a team that can do both.

You'll notice that I have restrained myself from relying too heavily on the concept of the CIO Paradox in this book. I cannot rely on that concept if I am to move on to new paradigms. But here, I cannot help myself. There is an essential contradiction between telling senior IT leadership teams that they always need a business sponsor and raising a generation of IT leaders who have the courage of their convictions. I see this paradox as the most potentially debilitating force in IT's ability to be the business.

CIOs who are breaking that paradox are baking courage into their formal leadership programs, or they are asking their teams to think like venture capitalists, or encouraging their people to get smart about other industries and "bring the outside in." But, as with any leadership challenge, it all starts at the top. Are you, as CIO, ready to stick your neck out a few inches more?

Chapter 6

Tell a Good Story

Since the beginning of time, people have loved to hear stories. "Tell me a story!" we would beg our parents when we were little. "Tell it again!"

To my mind, storytelling is one of the most important skills a CIO can possess. In the boardroom, the story is one of finance; in your IT leadership meetings, the story is one of vision, teamwork, and value; and with your customers, you tell a story of comfort, convenience, revenue, or happiness.

When two parties come from different backgrounds, they can struggle to share an understanding of something complex and abstract, like technology. CIOs, who bear the burden of educating a wide array of stakeholders about the cost, function, and business impact of technology, need a way to elucidate IT in a way that does not overwhelm, intimidate, or—heaven forfend—bore their audience.

"As CIOs, we need to demystify IT," says Malini Balakrishnan, former CIO of Building Materials Holding Corporation (BMC), a provider of building materials and construction services. "When current business executives were coming up through the ranks, technology was not as pervasive as it is today, so they were able to achieve success without having to understand it. Today, the reality is much different. As CIO, you don't want to preach to them, because that is a sure way to turn them off. You want to capture their interest by using analogies that they can identify with and that remind them of the challenges they face in their own business and their own lives."[1]

The Story of Mobility at JetBlue

JetBlue is aggressively pursuing a mobile strategy for pilots. "One way to introduce this kind of major IT program is to say, 'We're going to give tablets to everyone,'" says Eash Sundaram, JetBlue's EVP of innovation and CIO. "Then they respond, 'Why are we getting these tablets? Is this about keeping track of our hours on the job?' So, suddenly in IT, you are on the defensive."

The better way, according to Sundaram, is to tell the right story to these pilots, who all travel for a living: "We want you to be connected when you're in the plane. Think of this device as a connection to your office, but also to your family. Why carry two devices?"

"This way," Sundaram says, "you're reminding crew members of the importance of community and family; you're not pitching a device. The story is, 'If you want to sit in the lounge and check your bank statements, you can. If you want a video connection with your family, you can have it.'"

As IT leader at JetBlue, Sundaram spends a lot of time thinking about the benefits of having a device in the cockpit that allows pilots to do their jobs better and be happier crew members and about how to make those benefits a part of the story. "Most airlines have had major challenges deploying iPads in the flight deck; we've had only excitement. These other airlines think of the legalities, risk, complexity, and expense, but we think more broadly about how these technologies empower our crew members' quality of life. As CIO, I have to be able to sell that story."

A Movie Analogy at BMC

When Malini Balakrishnan arrived at BMC, she knew that the construction services company needed an ERP system. "With any organization, ERP rollouts can be tough, but in the lumber industry, where we run on razor-thin margins, new technology investments make executives nervous," says Balakrishnan. "Executives want to know, 'What is an ERP? Why do we need one? How much do I need to invest? How will this change what I do?'"

To preempt the fear and doubt that so often accompany technology-driven change, Balakrishnan told a story. "Think of our business as running on a fast-moving bus," Balakrishnan told her business partners. "We emerged from the housing slump in 2010, and now we are on an exciting journey to wonderful new destinations. We have great growth and great forward momentum, but the bus we are currently riding on is rickety and old; it will not get us to where we want to go."

Balakrishnan explained that the company needed a new bus that is faster and more fuel efficient, one that has GPS, Wi-Fi, and luxury seats. "But we cannot pull over, stop the old bus, and all transfer in an orderly fashion to this beautiful new bus. We need to keep the business running," she said. "So, we have to drive the old bus and simultaneously get the new bus ready. This means we will need to spend extra money, because we will be paying for the old bus and the new bus at the same time."

To drive her story home, Balakrishnan referenced the movie *Speed,* in which a young Keanu Reeves is a police officer in Los Angeles where maniacal Dennis Hopper, for some reason, has planted a bomb on a city bus. If the bus drops below 50 mph, it will explode. So, Keanu comes up with a plan to commission a second bus to run alongside the first one, and he encourages passengers to walk across a narrow plank from one bus to other. "We cannot slow our business down," Balakrishnan tells her peers. "At some point, we are going to have to move from one bus to the other," she says. "To make the transfer, the new bus has to be fully tested and working; we don't want to get on the new bus and then lose our forward momentum as a business."

In the movie, some passengers were afraid to get on the new bus because the transfer, walking across a gangplank, was too scary. So they stayed where they were and blew up. "In our business, many of our employees are nervous about the transition," Balakrishnan told her executive peers. "But we have to conquer the fear of transferring to the new bus. Just like the movie, staying on the old bus is not an option."

What the Business Didn't Ask for at Dr Pepper Snapple Group

In the new era of IT, when IT no longer enables business strategy, but instead informs and even defines it, CIOs no longer wait to be asked for requirements. They identify opportunities and define the technology solutions that will capitalize on those opportunities long before the business dreams up technology solutions on their own. This makes the CIO's ability to tell a good story all the more important, since the change that IT is proposing may come as a surprise to the businesses impacted most by it.

Dr Pepper Snapple Group (DPS) is a $6 billion producer and distributor of beverage products. The company sells much of its products through direct store delivery, which means that, every day, the sales force visits thousands of stores to take replenishment orders and pitch new products.

DPS also has account teams who work at a national level with retailers to develop programs and promotions for in-store events. Those programs have materials, collateral, displays, and pricing information, all of which need to be communicated to everyone involved in the program. If the Walmart account team at DPS, for example, creates a Dr Pepper football promotion for Walmart nationally, the reps need to get the right merchandise, products, and displays into all of the Walmart stores.

All of this means that, before the sales reps start their day, they need a list of the stores included in that day's route, order information on every account, collateral for promotions that have already been sold into the retail chain, and information about new promotions on offer. So, the IT team at DPS decided, proactively, to develop a solution to give the sales teams the information they needed.

Meeting a Challenge at DPS

For years, sales reps used printed materials to keep track of their routes and a hand-held device that only enabled them to take orders. "The reps carried product collateral around with them in binders," says Tom Farrah, who has been CIO of DPS since 2011. "The pages would be torn and out of date, and that's what they'd present to the customer. With just a few minutes to spend with the store manager, the rep could barely get a replenishment order filled, let alone execute on marketing promotions or sell new products."[2]

Without an efficient way to access all of that information, sales reps struggled. "There was a lot of finger pointing," says Farrah. "The sales people complained that they didn't know about current promotions and didn't have the right materials or relevant information. These are problems that we'd been discussing for years."

With the declining market for soda industry-wide, these issues were about more than finger pointing and morale; they had a direct impact on revenue.

"The reps had technology for order entry, and that was it," says Farrah. "We have hundreds of retail chains as customers. When our reps visit them, we want them to do more than take orders. We want them to sell."

Farrah and his IT team came up with a solution. "We developed MyDPS, an integrated suite of tools that we deliver over iPads," says Farrah. "What is unique about MyDPS is that, in addition to giving our reps mobile apps, we've built a huge back-end repository with a rules engine. A lot of companies give mobile apps to their reps, but nobody is really doing the big back-end piece with rules and content intelligence to make the information relevant to each sales person. That is what is makes MyDPS so successful."

With MyDPS, sales reps receive only the information about their own routes, accounts, and promotions. "If you are a sales rep for a branch that doesn't carry 7UP, you won't see any promotional information on 7UP," says Farrah. "If you don't service Kroger stores, you won't see information about Kroger activity. "

With MyDPS, every morning, sales reps click on a "My Day" button on their iPads, which connects to the back end and downloads everything they need for the day, including their routes, order information, and selling materials. When they open their browser, their home page is DPS's corporate intranet, which gives them only the corporate information relevant to their business role.

Selling the Solution Through Storytelling

Farrah and his team knew that they needed to sell the MyDPS concept to the sales organization, so they created drawings and mockups until they got to a point where they could tell a compelling story.

"We went to a number of sales meetings and delivered a 'day in the life of a sales rep' presentation,'" says Farrah. "We started the presentation with pictures of a rep walking into a store with a binder and a hand-held. Then we walked them through a series of 'what-ifs': What if the rep had an iPad? Great, he can do his e-mail. But what if he could take his orders on that device? What if he had a list of all of the promotions and prioritized activities that we want him to sell in to the account? What if he could click a button and bring up promotional materials that explain the benefits of the program, the pricing, and the profit margin? What if that information came to him every morning so that he can focus his time on selling?"

Farrah and his team visited DPS's five major businesses and presented the MyDPS concept. "We showed them what could be and we planted the seeds," he says. "The key was in talking about what the sales reps do now, and what they could be doing to maximize our incremental sales, which is our business objective. Their first priority is to take replenishment orders, but we want them to have an 'ask' to get the incremental sale."

Farrah's next step was to create a minipilot and give iPads to a small group of account reps. "We rigged up a temporary mechanism that downloaded materials from SharePoint. We faked it so that the reps could have the experience of the app." Farrah let the reps use the fake MyDPS for a month and then asked that business's president to meet with the reps who had been using the pilot. "The president and I had a roundtable discussion with the reps," says Farrah. "We let them talk about how the app was working, and then we went with them to a customer, where they demoed how they were using it. The reps told us some great stories about how having those materials helped them with an incremental sell."

Once that president was sold on MyDPS, Farrah was able to get buy-in from a number of additional general managers and sales leaders, all of whom began to see real results. "We are in a direct store delivery business, which is all about selling," says Farrah. "We need to stock the stores, provide merchandizing, and sell to them as efficiently as possible. Now, our sales reps can sell better because they have the right story and the facts. That's a huge advantage."

For Farrah and his team, delivering MyDPS was anything but an order-taking activity. "Nobody in our business asked for MyDPS," says Farrah. "We developed the concept in IT and then got buy-in. IT drove the whole thing. As CIO, I know that part of IT's job is to fulfill requests, but our real job is to understand the business and come up with innovative ideas."

Telling a story about change means taking a risk: when the IT team pushes forward with a system that no one in the business requested, they are sticking their necks out. "If you are willing to take risks and think about problems you can solve for your business, then you just have to have the guts to go do it," says Farrah. "You have to believe in it and sell it. Selling it is not just showing ROI; it is showing your business a real problem and how to solve it."

A Pie Chart Story at Adobe Systems

The first article I ever wrote for *CIO* magazine, way back in 1999, was about "demonstrating IT value." How, I asked our readership, can CIOs change the conversation about IT from one of cost to one of value? Here we are, seventeen years later (and yet I haven't changed a bit!), wrestling with the same challenge.

When Gerri Martin-Flickinger was CIO of Adobe Systems, she worked hard to change the story of IT in her company. "My business leaders didn't spend a lot of time thinking about IT legacy debt," Martin-Flickinger says. "So, I worked very hard to separate for them what is legacy and what is strategic. To me, that is what a good CIO does."[3]

A few years ago, Martin-Flickinger had a revelation: "We were using all of these complex financial models to report on how we were spending our IT dollars, but the model was too complicated to tell the right story." In particular, Martin-Flickinger was finding that her executive peers glossed over the role that depreciation plays in the IT budget.

"I had to get my business partners to realize that the projects we do today have a large capitalized component that will show up as operations expenses for the next five years," she says. "Those costs can stack up like stair steps: a little money this year, and a little money next year. If you don't keep an eye on depreciation, it can overtake the rest of your OpEx budget very rapidly."

Martin-Flickinger realized that, as with so many things in IT, simplest was best. While she continued to use complex financial models to determine IT spend, she changed the presentation of those numbers to something very simple. "I started using a pie chart that had only three sections: operations, new delivery, and depreciation," Martin-Flickinger says. The dashboard was concise and clearly illustrated the impact that IT had on the business. "This made a major difference with my CEO," she says.

Once she started putting the pie chart on every dashboard and report she gave to the executive committee, Martin-Flickinger noticed a change: "Every time I went in to talk to the executives, I brought that pie chart with me. I found that the dialogue changed to focus on the three parts of the budget."

Thanks to the pie chart, Adobe's executive team now understands the costs of IT, the value of IT, and the role that depreciation plays. "The pie chart solution sounds so simple," says Martin-Flickinger. "But for me, it was the secret sauce in focusing our executives on how we are spending our IT budget."

Every CIO I have ever known has told me that his or her first order of business when starting a new CIO job was establishing trust between the business and IT. Trust is so hard won, but so easily lost, that when it sits on the shaky foundation of systems, infrastructure, training, and vendors, it is very difficult to establish for the long term. Yet, trust with the business is critical to any successful IT organization; here is where storytelling really comes in handy.

A Story of Cultural Change

When Jay Ferro became CIO of the American Cancer Society in 2012, IT had little credibility in the organization and was moving from a decentralized to a centralized structure.

"We were bringing together all of the functions in thirteen different organizations, each with its own leadership and technology, and IT was going first," says Ferro. "I had to build our business's confidence in a department that they felt was in great need of improvement and rally an organization about to go through major change."[4]

To start the process, Ferro met with his IT staff and a large number of IT's constituents to formulate a path to a better place and to develop a new story of IT, based on the following four key tenets.

Tell the Truth and Give the Facts

To Ferro, establishing a fact-based mindset is the most important pillar of the four. "Whether we are talking about outages, customer support, business goals, or outcomes, we are talking metrics, not emotion," he says.

As a case in point, one of the American Cancer Society's key applications is its customer relationship management system, which captures data on tens of millions of donors. "Everything we do flows through that system," says Ferro. "I said, 'Let's break down the problems and get to the heart of what was going wrong. Could you not log in? What is slow? Do you need more training?' Within a few weeks of deliberate conversation, we came out with eight facts that would help us make significant improvements. We knew that, if we upgraded those areas, the system would work better for everyone."

Ferro noted that the American Cancer Society is an evidence-based organization, and as such, its leaders make research and program decisions on the basis of research. But the IT organization was making decisions on the basis of influence, emotion, and morale. "We changed all of that," says Ferro. "Now, we start with basic metrics: uptime, customer satisfaction, and throughput," he says. To underscore the fact-based approach, Ferro uses a combination of COBIT, ITIL, ISO, and other delivery standards for IT.

"We don't subscribe to one standard overall; we use best of breed," he says. "But when you are having fact-based conversations and then you tie your delivery practices to industry standards, you are reinforcing the fact-based approach. This is not just 'Jay's way'; this is the industry's way."

Live Our Values

Ferro asked a group in his IT organization—directors and below—to develop a new set of IT values, and they came up with "IT CODE," an acronym for "integrity, teamwork, communication, ownership, dedication, and excellence."

"The IT CODE is baked into our objectives; my team and I are incented on it," says Ferro. The American Cancer Society also gives an IT CODE award to IT staffers nominated by employees in IT and other business areas. "Our new CEO will recognize our IT CODE winner at our next all-staff meeting," says Ferro. "I'll give the winner a gift card, a plaque, and all of that, but when your CEO thanks an IT person for a job well done, it's pretty powerful."

Empower and Include

To Ferro, "IT cannot be an island, especially when you are going through a huge transformation." Some of Ferro's key partners right out of the gate were the talent strategy group, corporate communications, and legal. "I went straight to our chief talent officer to share our talent strategy and to ask for feedback," he says. "And I worked with our head of corporate communications on our IT CODE communication plan." Ferro even turned some IT functions over to his business partners.

"We built a new IT PMO, which, three years later, has a dotted line to me and a solid line to our EPMO. And our IT finance group is in the finance organization. Sometimes inclusion means letting go."

When Ferro first took the job, he heard that the office of the CIO was shrouded in secrecy and that only the CIO could provide budgetary approval. To change this, he pushed decision rights and budget authority down into the organization as far as he could. "We were very open about our budget, and we delegated approval authority incrementally," he says. "Now, a much larger percentage of IT people can make decisions about training and purchasing; we eliminated a lot of the red tape and bureaucracy."

Share and Communicate

"Every CIO should have a formal communication plan with a library of materials to share at a moment's notice," says Ferro. "But to us, sharing and communication means something more." Ferro and his fellow executives talk openly with IT about the mission of the American Cancer Society and how the organization is doing against its goals. "Three years ago, only 20 percent of the IT organization participated in our mission through donations and volunteering at our events," he says. "Today, that number is over 95 percent."

To Ferro, this kind of participation in the society's mission gives the IT organization credibility and forces it to use its own fundraising and volunteer coordination technology.

Blogging the Story at Mylan

Michael Smith is a big fan of the "share and communicate" concept. Smith, now global head of digital and innovation and global business services, became CIO of Mylan in 2012, five years after the pharmaceutical company had acquired Merck's generic drug business. The fifty-year-old company had become a large global company in only five years and had work to do to fully integrate the acquisition, tear down silos, and establish global processes.

With huge transformation ahead of them, Smith saw that the IT organization was lacking some basic communication tools necessary to drive change. "We were a company that needed to scale to the next level, but we did not have the technology to allow our executives to send consistent messages throughout the company," he says.[5]

The IT team was also about to experience change. "I walked into an IT organization that was not in the best shape," says Smith. "We had no enterprise architecture, no centralized infrastructure group, no business intelligence, and no digital capabilities," he says. What's more, like so many CIOs inheriting an IT organization, Smith found that IT had outsourced the wrong functions. "Our resource model was backward," says Smith. "The commodity work was done in house, and the strategic work was done outside."

On the verge of a major reengineering effort of its global business processes and a comprehensive restructuring of the IT organization and sourcing model, Smith needed to tell a new story of IT to his organization and to the broader business community. To do that, he needed a better communication tool than e-mail. So, with the help of the VP of communications at Mylan, Smith started a blog. "The beauty of the blog was that I was able to be transparent about where we were going and why," Smith says. "The blog turned out to be a fantastic change management tool."

During most IT reorganizations, people get very nervous as the CIO pulls the IT leadership team into closed door meetings. "I decided to use the blog to hit that issue head on," says Smith. "I knew that people were aware that the top fifteen leaders were heading to an offsite, so I used the blog to let everyone know what our offsite goals were. I tried to make sure we were clear about our goals for restructuring and how we were going to get there." Smith believes his blog strategy has paid off. "Morale has stayed high during the restructuring, and the buzz around the IT organization is good," he says.

Not only has the blog helped quell nerves associated with the restructuring in IT, it enables Smith and his leadership team to communicate effectively with the rest of the business. "At one point, we posted an animated five-minute video to show how our IT strategy connects to our business strategy," says Smith. "As CIOs, we are in the unique position of communicating to the rest of the company how the IT and the business strategy are linked," he says. "The blog helps me to do that. You can't find anyone in the company who doesn't understand our IT strategy or anyone in IT who doesn't understand our business strategy."

Smith is not the only person to use the blog. "The blog has changed the way we communicate as a company," says Smith. "Anyone in the company who wants to talk about something has a platform to do it." In addition to giving voice to employees, the blog helps management understand how well employees are handling change. "With the blog, we can see what employees are thinking about and how the reaction to the transformation is trending," says Smith. "The blog allows us to be sensitive to our employees and gives us a new level of understanding about our direction."

Conclusion

When IT moves from enabling business strategy to defining it, the story of IT needs to change. IT is not an expensive but necessary evil. IT does not wait around to be told what to do. IT is consultative and proactive and drives innovation, value, and results. Recasting IT's role and delivering a steady stream of new solutions to your business requires major oratorical talent. You will not change hearts and minds through architectural diagrams, and architectural diagrams will not help you to get others to carry your message forward. Whether it's a movie, a football game, a military exercise, or a parenting experience, people love stories—and they love to retell them. Stories are the most powerful communication devices that we have. Become a better storyteller and you will become a better CIO.

Chapter 7

Grow Blended Executives

When IT enables business strategy, CIOs need people in their organizations who can understand a set of business requirements and deliver on them. When IT defines business strategy, CIOs need so much more. To my mind, there is no harder task than moving an IT organization from order takers to order shapers, and asking a team of technologists, whose tool set undergoes a paradigm shift every eighteen months or so, to be strategic, consultative, customer focused, *and* delightful.

At the root of the talent problem is the fact that, while technology deployments and business process improvements are two sides of the same coin—each informing the other—people don't grow up that way.

People either grow up in IT or they grow up outside of IT, and by the time they are at the director level, they tend to know their discipline very well (marketing systems *or* supply chain processes *or* network architecture *or* compliance regulations), but that's all they know.

What we need are what I call "blended executives"—professionals with subject-matter expertise both in a technology area and in a functional discipline or business process. But here's the rub: companies are not growing these blended executives in any kind of consistent, programmatic way. Some companies, mostly very large ones, do have rotational programs that send IT people into other functional areas and "business people" into IT, and these programs typically work great. But the majority of companies, because of bureaucracy, culture, resources, or a combination of these factors, do not.

The CIOs of these companies need to find creative approaches to growing blended executives, or IT will continue to enable rather than lead. IT will "partner with" the business or "support" the business, but IT will not "be" or lead the business. The challenge of growing blended executives involves much more than teaching business skills to technologists. This is a new era of IT, which brings with it not only changes in technology, business strategy, customer engagement, and the like; it also brings a perspective change, a mental shift in how we understand our value and our relationship to our work.

"We have to get away from the idea that career trajectories should be measured by how large an organization a person has managed in terms of teams and assets owned by the company," says Jeff Donaldson, who spent years as head of IT and of innovation at GameStop, the $9 billion retail gaming company, and who has recently retired. "In the future IT organization, leaders will manage assets owned by external partners. A career should be measured by the value a person delivers to the company, not by what they own."[1]

For Victor Fetter, CIO of LPL Financial, the future CIO will need a balanced skill-set. "The next generation of senior IT leaders needs to possess both a strategic vision and a focus on operational excellence," he says. "They also need to have a competency around relationship management that allows them to talk to a deep-rooted engineer one day and a business professional, or the market, the next. It's about the well-rounded individual, not someone who comes out of one core discipline."

As we discussed in chapter 3, on dismantling the iceberg, the technology supply chain has gone through dramatic change. In the olden days, you would sign a deal with one or two major vendors who would supply you a suite of packaged systems. Selecting and managing those vendors wasn't easy, but it was relatively straightforward. But with the new era of IT, "we live in a different world," says Gerri Martin-Flickinger, former CIO of Adobe. "You need to stay tight with venture capital firms. You need to understand what the next disruptors are going to be. You need to be confident that the company you're doing business with today is actually innovating for tomorrow. When those technical supply chain partners break down or can't deliver, or have a weakness in their chain, it affects everything. It's a very interdependent model."

This means that, in addition to embracing the concept of partner-led initiatives, and balancing vision and delivery, future IT leaders need to be able to broker and integrate a fleet of third-party players. "We now have an interdependent technology supply chain, says Martin-Flickinger. "We need people who know how to integrate, in all senses of the word, with third-party companies, broker those relationships, hold everybody accountable to resolve issues, but—as importantly—stay close to them for their next-generation products."

Personal Attributes

Being the business involves, first and foremost, a perspective change, so it makes good sense to identify what new perspective you want your senior leadership team to possess. The more you understand that perspective, the better you can seek out the personal attributes that will support it, and the faster you will develop a culture that will thrive in the new era of IT. These days, IT professionals hail from marketing, finance, IT, and pretty much every other department in a company. Having a well-defined set of overriding personal attributes will allow you to build an effective culture, regardless of background or skill-set.

Jeff Donaldson has identified some of the personal attributes he has looked for when hiring for the technology organization at GameStop:

- **Value trumps size.** How large a team have you managed? How big is your budget? We in the executive search business are repeatedly guilty of assessing talent by metrics—the bigger, the better. This has to change, according to Donaldson. Empire building is out. After all, in the world of cloud services and crowdsourcing, most of an IT leader's resources exist somewhere outside of the company. "You will be relying more and more on assets that you procure," Donaldson says. "If you're going to be a great collaborative leader, you need to stop counting owned assets."

- **Get comfortable with "not invented here."** Most companies have been outsourcing for years now, but IT organizations are still rife with managers who believe that if you can't touch it, you can't manage it. "We need leaders who are happy to use someone else's work to deliver value to their company," says Donaldson. "You don't have to create everything in-house. It is far more effective to use public APIs and components off the shelf. If you are going to take advantage of partnerships, you have to lose the mentality that you have to develop your solutions yourself. By relying on the work of others, you'll move faster."

- **Be data driven.** Some executives are comfortable basing their decisions on new, unstructured, and unconventional forms of data, but many are not. Part of the change that IT needs to lead is creating a data-driven culture throughout the business. Being data driven doesn't mean that everyone in IT needs a degree in data science, but "today, all of our businesses are data driven, and as an IT leader, you have to develop the mindset that everyone in the company is making decisions through data," says Donaldson. "These could be decisions about delivering customer value, your changing marketplace, or the optimal cost structure for your business. But whatever the issues, gut feel is no longer enough."

Donaldson never expected his IT leaders to spend their days with their heads buried in spreadsheets, but he did expect that "they will have enough knowledge to understand the instrumentation needed to collect data, the mechanisms by which data is stored and accessed, and the techniques that are typically used to analyze that data."

- **Have a human-centered sense of design.** To Donaldson, this might be the most important attribute of all. "Whether we are delivering a product to employees or to customers, human-centered design will become fundamental to what we do. We have to have that talent in our companies."

CBRE's Mandy Edwards has boiled the attributes she looks for and develops in her senior team down to four:

- **Business acumen.** While understanding CBRE's business and how it works is important, Edwards looks for more: "Our IT leaders need to bring in other industry perspectives that we can leverage in our business," she says.

- **Risk management.** "Risk in the IT organization comes in many different flavors," says Edwards. "I rely on my team's ability to balance risk when they make decisions."

• **Decision making.** "There are great engineers who become immobilized by too many technology choices," Edwards says. "I value the skill of being able to make a decision and move forward."

• **Navigating the technology landscape.** How do senior leaders stay informed about new technologies? Do they participate in industry associations? Have they built a vast network of really good technology people over the years? "Whatever it is," says Edwards, "I want them to have an effective approach to navigating new technologies."

Julia Anderson, CIO of Smithfield Foods, adds another attribute to the list—wanting to make a difference. "Sometimes IT people fall in love with technology, vendors, and three letter acronyms," she says. "That makes it hard for them to find the right solution. We need our people to fall in love with making a difference to the business. They need to be excited about getting closer to their business partners and finding ways to solve their problems. Go on plant tours; go to the warehouse; talk to everyone. That's the only way to see that having seventeen different ways to print labels is something we need to fix."

Once you know the personal attributes you are hiring for, you need an effective way to assess those skills in your candidate pool, and that starts with the interview.

The Interview

Take it from someone who has spent more than a decade prepping candidates for interviews and then hearing interview feedback, the interview is an inefficient tool for assessing talent, but it is entrenched. Many companies ask finalists to take behavioral assessments, develop case studies, and make presentations, all of which go a long way toward ensuring a good fit, but the interview is still the first step in the process. The more strategic you are in interviewing candidates, the more quickly you can identify the personal attributes you are looking for.

"I never talk to candidates about their CVs," says Dan Olley, EVP of product development and CTO of Elsevier, the global information solutions provider. "They can write and I can read; we know that." Rather than focus on skills and experiences, Olley interviews for two raw capabilities: "Clear thinkers—people who can cut through day-to-day ambiguity to create clarity on how to move forward; and strategic pragmatists—people who are strategic enough to make a plan but pragmatic enough to know that they might not implement all of it."[2]

Olley breaks his interviews into six areas of focus: technology, process and practice, talent acquisition and development, leadership, commercial acumen, and personal efficiency. He asks a high-level question first, and if the candidate offers a solid repose, he'll drill down for detail.

For commercial acumen, for example, Olley starts with something basic. "You would be amazed by how many people with big jobs can't answer some basic gating questions, like the real difference between CapEx and OpEx," he says.

Should a candidate survive the CapEx and OpEx question, Olley follows up: How does CapEx actually hit the P&L? Walk me through that process. Explain whether it would be good or bad to capitalize an internal full-time employee. Why? "I'm looking for a deep understanding of these financial mechanisms," says Olley. "I'm peeling back the layers. It's one thing to understand basic financial terms, but how deeply does the candidate understand how these financial processes actually work?"

When assessing technology depth, Olley might ask candidates to discuss the difference between a traditional relational database and a

NoSQL repository. "If they can answer that question, I'll ask them when they would use each," he says. "What would be the key drivers? I want to know that they truly understand the concepts and can apply them."

When it comes to leadership, Olley focuses on change. He asks candidates to talk about an example of where they've led change and what they've learned from it. "When you talk to people about change, they usually talk about leading a reorganization," he says. "But that's the most basic kind of change. I'm looking for something deeper."

Olley recalls a candidate who did very well in the discussion about change. "He told me that the business was hemorrhaging, and they knew they needed to change. He talked about changing the very core of his company's business model, altering the product release schedule to help users through the change, and building change right into the product. He spoke about change at every level." That candidate demonstrated to Olley that he was a change leader in the way that he thought about the world. "Rather than say, 'I reorganized the team,'" says Olley, "he showed me that he understood that his job, in every dimension, is about change."

Keeping IT Focused on Business Goals

After the merger between NSTAR Electric and Gas and Northeast Utilities in 2014, Kathy Kountze-Tatum, who was formerly CIO of NSTAR, became CIO of the new $7 billion gas and electric utility (now called Eversource Energy) and she was ready to transform IT.

Kountze-Tatum had recently completed two major steps toward that transformation: She had outsourced a huge number of the non-core operational functions that had previously been performed by her team. And she had restructured her new two-hundred-person IT organization to allow her team to play much more strategic roles.

While implementing a new sourcing model and designing a strategic organization are Herculean efforts to be sure, they are only the beginning. "We'd been so thoroughly heads down and transitioning to our new organization model, we hadn't spent enough time talking about how to help transform the company going forward," Kountze-Tatum says. "Our new IT organization was positioned to be highly strategic. But positioning and being are two different things." Kountze-Tatum's entire business case for outsourcing was that the people retained in IT would be strategic and solution oriented. "We had said it, we'd written it, and we had the buy-in and support; now we had to do it," she says.[3]

Kountze-Tatum decided to hold a two-day meeting with the senior leaders of her brand-new IT organization to assess their readiness for their new strategic role. "We had just come out of a very complicated transition, and we needed time to focus on issues besides day to day," she says. "This meeting was an opportunity to do some forward thinking about how to achieve our ultimate goal: to walk beside our business partners—not behind them or in front of them—and show the value that strong IT professionals can bring to an organization."

On day one, Kountze-Tatum had some of her newly positioned leaders report on the strategies for their area. "Now that we had outsourced the day-to-day support of our infrastructure, I needed our infrastructure leader to talk to me about what our strategy in that area should be going forward," she says. "What are our priorities? We have the support structure to get to a better place, but what is our strategy for making that happen? I needed to learn if everyone truly understood that we were a new organization that needed to think and operate differently."

During the team's review of their future plans in each area, Kountze-Tatum listened for a new perspective on IT's role. "Even though we were still responsible for the technical piece, I needed my team to understand that our solutions should be based on operating model changes, not just technical requirements," she says. "Do they think about what is changing in HR as we support a new SaaS solution? Are they considering customer care's long-term vision as we rethink our web environment?"

On day two, the topic was staffing. "We had this new organizational model in place so that we could be consulting partners to our business partners," says Kountze-Tatum. "But were we staffed correctly? Did we have the right roles performing the right duties?" Kountze-Tatum found, for example, that her team was struggling with understanding exactly what architects should be doing now: focusing solely on building roadmaps, doing more collaborative work with business analysts, or both?

Changing any IT organization from technical specialists to process change consultants is tough because the new role requires so much balance. You certainly don't want them to be order takers, where they limit their contribution to implementing technology selected by others. But you also don't want them to go too far and make all of the technology decisions themselves.

"We've had experiences where our business partners say 'IT made that decision' when things go wrong," says Kountze-Tatum. "I had to get my team to recognize the balancing act that it takes to be consultative. Even though they participate in the business operational discussions, they still need a business sponsor on these projects 100 percent. Sometimes, I have to pull my people back and say, 'Ask the right questions, listen, and add your perspective, but the ultimate decisions about the business operating model is not yours.'"

The "IT as order taker" challenge is one that Herman De Prins, CIO of UCB, the $4.2 billion pharmaceutical company, set out to overcome when he designed a program called "The Future of IT." De Prins had been reading articles that declared that cloud and digital technologies would push IT to the margins, so he decided to change the culture in IT. "I knew that if we stuck to traditional IT at UCB, we would be in a negative cycle of cost cutting and reduced relevance," he says.[4]

Here is how De Prins described the program to participants: "This program will help participants understand how to meet new expectations for their role. These new expectations start with accountability: IT employees need to do more than implement what is requested. They need to ensure the right choices are made and the expected business value is achieved. To do so, IT employees need to build strategic relationships with their business partners. This requires good subject-matter expertise and the courage to initiate or engage in discussions about relevant business problems."

Central to the Future of IT program at UCB are five pillars that De Prins embeds into every meeting, employee review, and career path discussion:

• **Quality.** The IT team at UCB has always focused on quality, but De Prins established quality as a pillar to emphasize its importance as demand and cost pressures increase. He cites UCB's collaboration technologies as a case in point. "We have nine thousand employees at UCB, and we run four hundred thousand scheduled video-enabled conferences over our own network every year. In this kind of environment, we cannot jeopardize quality. So, if someone on the network team tells me, 'I can lower the cost of our networks by making a few changes,' my response is, 'Great! But what impact does that change have on our quality?'"

• **Specialization.** There is considerable debate among CIOs about whether to develop technology professionals as generalists or specialists. De Prins comes down clearly on the side of specialization. "I want everyone to be a specialist, whether it's in Java or analytics or mobility," he says. "Technology is ubiquitous and more intense than ever. That means that IT people cannot know a little about a lot. They need enough depth about a technology area that they can contribute significantly to a discussion about solutions and capabilities. With specialization comes the need for having many experiences, to create 'T-shaped' individuals. That's why development is critical."

For example, the IT organization at UCB considers SAP to be a mature technology, so when a position is open in the SAP group, they do not look outside for someone with SAP expertise. Instead, they pull someone from another team into SAP and teach him that skill. Then they fill the open headcount with someone who has specialization in a new domain, like digital or analytics. "This way, we are always developing people and bringing in new areas of specialization," De Prins says.

• **Work as a team.** If you are going to build an organization filled with specialists, you must establish a strong foundation of collaboration. "When you are a specialist, you cannot know it all," says De Prins. "So you have to get very good at collaborating with people inside of IT, outside of IT, and third parties."

De Prins organizes IT by functional domains, including research, development, commercial operations, and technical operations. "Some IT people have depth in a function, and others have depth in a specific technology area," says De Prins. "When it comes to analytics, we cannot put that capability in every function, because we have only one group of analytics specialists. This means that our analytics people need to team up with domain specialists. Teamwork has to be one of our pillars."

• **Hatch the egg.** "We all think a lot about innovation and how to generate innovative ideas," says De Prins. "But if the innovation takes too long to develop, it's usually not worth it." Rather than spend an eternity thinking things through, De Prins wants his team to take action. To get his team to hatch the egg, De Prins has a process. He runs forums on analytics and mobility in which members brainstorm ideas. "We ask the forums to produce a high volume of new ideas, and then we give them fifty days to explore," he says. "After fifty days, we review the ideas and select those that seem viable in terms of value, cost, and time to market. We then give the people behind that smaller group of ideas another fifty days to add more data to support the idea's viability. 'Hatch the egg,' as a pillar, emphasizes the importance of brainstorming a lot of ideas, but evaluating them quickly and getting the best to market fast."

• **Market your value.** "We deliver on two hundred projects a year in IT, and we need to engage in some self-promotion," says De Prins. "But only when you talk about business value, do you get any appreciation for what you do. If I say I manage three thousand servers that don't go down, that tells the business very little. But if I tell them that we ensure patient safety and access to medicine because our systems are fault tolerant (and by the way those systems run on three thousand servers), then I am marketing our value, not just our activity."

Opportunistic Rotation

When it comes to changing perspectives, there is nothing as powerful as walking a mile in someone else's shoes. Placing application developers in infrastructure roles creates better developers. Inviting marketing professionals to do some time in IT makes for a much better business partner, and exporting IT leaders into non-IT business functions cultivates those blended skills that we all need so desperately on our teams. So, why don't all companies have mature and well-run rotational programs? Usually, it's because the demands on

IT are so great that IT organizations can barely take a breath, let alone lend leaders to other functions or train new imports.

If you do not have the resources or wherewithal for a formal rotation program, keep your eye out for single opportunities to do some trading.

When Marc Franciosa (now CIO of LyondellBasell) became CIO of Praxair, a $11 billion industrial gases company, both the business and the IT organization ran on a federated model, with regional businesses making their own decisions about data centers, architecture, application development, and IT strategy. "This approach let the regions be nimble, but it didn't allow us to replicate processes and drive global change," says Franciosa. "If we had a best practice in a region, it was difficult even to recognize it as a best practice, let alone scale it to our other regional businesses."[5]

So, Franciosa balanced the regional vs. global focus and created globalized IT functions around strategy, architecture, infrastructure, application development, and program management, with regional resources to build relationships between IT and the regions, and to manage local vendors.

The new organizational model made good sense for Praxair, but having taken the majority of IT resources out of the businesses, Franciosa ran the risk of having a "technology focused" team too disconnected from the businesses it supported. "When you're always focused on technology, and your team is busy running operations and designing architectures, they are not learning about the business," he says.

To address this, Franciosa knew he needed to develop blended executives who understood both IT and some major aspect of Praxair's business functions. Rather than build a formal rotational program, he looked for singular opportunities to cultivate a blended skill-set.

Franciosa had an IT leader who was very effective in one of Praxair's largest regional businesses. He knew that this leader had the capacity to learn more about the business, especially finance, so he considered rotating her into finance and then bringing her back into IT. But he found a better strategy. "We actually moved our finance function (for this same large regional business) under her in IT," he says. "Now, in addition to her work in IT, she is responsible for accounts payable, treasury, and tax for the regional businesses she knows so well."

Franciosa admits that moving a finance function into the IT organization is out of the box, but in taking the risk, he wound up "developing an executive with a deep understanding of two major areas of our business," he says.

Another example of "opportunistic blending" involved Praxair's pricing team. "We had someone in the pricing function who had been in the role for many years and had deep knowledge of how we priced all of our products and services," he says. "He was comfortable with our legacy pricing systems, but he did not know our new ERP."

So Franciosa moved this pricing person into the IT organization, to lead the pricing work-stream for Praxair's global ERP implementation. "In learning the new platform, he also learned a new way to do pricing," says Franciosa. "His ERP work has made him much stronger in his functional area." In addition, the ERP work allowed this executive to learn business functions beyond pricing, including credit collections, product hierarchy, and more. "By moving this person from the business into IT, we broadened his business knowledge and built out his technology acumen," Franciosa says.

When seizing on opportunities to develop blended executives, Franciosa has some advice: "People will tell you why it can't be done. They will tell you, 'You can't expect a business person to become a technologist,' or 'You're going to take an IT person and teach them collections?' You have to have a little bit of courage when making these changes."

Moving business people into IT, or IT people into the business, has the obvious benefit of allowing you to grow blended executives. But, according to Franciosa, there is an additional advantage. "All of these people now have a greater appreciation for the connection between IT and business processes and in the end are integral to driving business results," he says. "And they can build great relationships as a result. They become advocates for the IT organization."

Conclusion

When I first started out in IT leadership executive search more than a decade ago, I created a "rock star" tag in my database. These exceptional creatures would be my go-to candidates whenever I launched a new search. Who qualified for the coveted rock star status? Strategists, influencers, and leaders of change, of course! Whether or not they had deep technology skills was of less interest to me. My clients (mostly CIOs at the time) needed talent who knew the business and could partner with its leaders. But, after completing a year's worth of searches for VPs of App Dev, infrastructure, and chief architects, I got wise. Candidates with soft skills alone, I found, were not that hard to find; what my CIO clients were after were the candidates with deep technology skills. Now, I have come to realize it is both. My rock star tag (which I apply very selectively) is reserved for that beautiful unicorn, the executive who has it all: relationship building, delivery excellence, deep technology roots, strategic thinking, and depth in whatever industry my client represents. These gorgeous creatures have the blended skill-set that will help them to lead the perspective change that the new era of IT demands.

If you, as CIO, would like to hire my firm and tap into my rock star database, my team thanks you, my husband thanks you, and I thank you. But you would be far wiser to develop the culture, vision, and rotational programs to grow your own.

Chapter 8

Be the Business

You know the story: your internal business partners have a technology need, but they decide that the IT department is too slow. So they retreat to the shadows, hire their own development shop, and commission new applications. You are willing to look the other way, until something with performance goes terribly wrong. Then it's your job to step in and scale, secure, or save the applications. If only you had been involved from the start...

Ten years ago, the term "shadow IT" described the staff that your business partners hired to build or support their own solutions. But now, as cloud services technology has made it relatively easy for your business partners to purchase their own technology, shadow IT is a much larger concept. When a vendor has a new database marketing product that your SVP of marketing decides to adopt without your knowledge, that's shadow IT. When your head of sales rolls out her own instance of Salesforce.com, that's shadow IT. In fact, a few months ago, I met with the sales team of an up-and-coming SaaS provider who told me that they did their best to do an end run around the CIO and go straight to the finance, HR, or sales teams to make the sale. That's shadow IT as well.

But shadow IT is a concept that should find no purchase in the new era of IT. When technology has become as important to a company as people, or finance, or even oxygen, the "us and them" divide between IT and its business partners has to go. When technology belongs to everyone, the IT organization needs to relinquish its totalitarian grasp over the purchase, development, and support of technology. Technology does not belong to the IT organization alone, and CIOs must figure out how to decrease their team's need to clamp down on rogue business leaders. If IT is going to be the business, then we must let the business be IT.

"We call it business unit technology, not shadow IT," says Matt Speare, CIO of Regions Bank. "We had to reframe our thought process in IT and realize that, if you try to centralize everything, you increase the time it takes to get things done. We had to start thinking of our business partners as an extended part of our technology family."

Part of the challenge in reframing IT's thinking around shadow IT is that IT people are risk averse. And who can blame them? They are responsible for availability, performance, and disaster recovery, along with little things, like data security. Allowing end users to develop technology is anathema to the risk management mandate in IT.

"Within our consumer bank, our e-business group has resources for design and user experience development, resources that my staff always believed should be in IT," says Speare. "But we have come to see that the e-business people are creative thinkers who need the freedom to innovate. So now we let them develop their own technology, but we guide them in making sure their rich web designs won't cause infrastructure issues when we put them in front of two million customers."

Let the Business Be IT

The IT team at Freddie Mac has developed an architectural solution to shadow IT. When Rob Lux joined Freddie Mac as CIO in 2010, he received a report that said the company had more than two thousand "end-user computing applications" (EUCs), which are applications that end users commissioned themselves. "The attitude in IT was, 'OK business, you can have your EUCs, but you're on your own,'" says Lux." 'If something bad happens, deal with it yourself.'"[1]

Attitude notwithstanding, IT would inevitably step in when an EUC that had become critical to the business was unable to scale. Beset by performance crisis, the EUC owner told IT that they needed to "productionalize" the app, that is, reengineer it for enterprise scale. This situation was stressful for both IT and the business.

The senior IT leadership team considered the strategy of hiring a firm to reverse engineer the EUCs into enterprise applications but quickly rejected that idea. "Converting EUCs to apps is like draining the lake as the river fills it up on the other end," says Lux. "People will keep building new EUCs, and the vendors leading the reengineering effort would have employment for life."

Instead, the IT team prioritized the different EUCs they discovered and brought the critical applications out of the shadows. They made sure that those apps had support, disaster recovery, security, and everything else that a big app needs. But Lux's team decided the same level of centralized control wasn't needed for the smaller, non-critical EUCs.

Once the IT team relented on centralized control, they came up with an innovative idea: build an enterprise platform for EUCs, and instead of converting the EUCs to applications, migrate them to the platform. New EUCs, regardless of who did the development, would be built on the enterprise platform as well.

"If people need an app to do a little piece of their work that isn't critical to our business or isn't SOX related, why do we care?" Lux says. "Why do we need to control everything? Let's let them do their jobs."

Lux and his team devised a three-step plan toward building the new platform. The first step was documenting all of the EUCs in use. Here, they were in good shape, because Freddie Mac already required EUC owners to register their apps in a central repository. So IT didn't have to spend a lot of time on this first, critical step of documentation.

The IT department had also completed a comprehensive inventory of EUCs. "They thought, 'No other firm has this many EUCs!'" says Lux. "I told them that I had worked in companies that had just as many EUCs as Freddie Mac. But because they didn't do an inventory, they may not have realized it at the time."

The next step was to determine which technologies the EUCs used as a prelude to developing a managed platform where they could reside. "If your business's managed applications are using very diverse technologies, you will need to determine whether you can standardize on just a few and convert the others," says Lux. Fortunately, the EUCs at Freddie Mac tended to use SaaS and the Microsoft stack, so building a managed platform was relatively straightforward.

The third and most important step, of course, was building trust between the business units and IT. As a part of establishing that trust, IT set up an EUC governance group designed to bring IT closer to the business units in collaborating on new functionality. "Sometimes you have shadow IT because the business unit just doesn't want to deal with IT," Lux says. "If they trusted IT, they would never have built the EUCs in the first place."

Freddie Mac's IT department launched this three-step plan, and within eighteen months, the percentage of critical EUCs running on its managed platform increased from 8 percent to 77 percent. "This does not mean that IT manages these apps," says Lux. "IT manages the platform they sit on. Through that platform, we can guarantee that the apps have backup, disaster recovery, and data encryption, but the EUC owners can make their own modifications."

Lux and his team are very happy with the EUC platform, the way it brought end users out of the shadows and readied them to partner with IT. But Lux says there is still work to do. "We want to get to a point where there is no distinction between an app and an EUC. But for now, our business units know their IT department is not out to shut down EUCs. IT is just here to support our business."

When you let go of the notion that IT must control all technology development, you have the potential to open the floodgates on innovation. "The traditional CIO mindset has always been 'It's my silo and you can't come in,'" says Eash Sundaram, EVP of innovation and CIO of JetBlue. "But IT is no longer a skillet; it's a tool kit, and my job as CIO is to give everyone access to the tool kit. When you build a platform that allows you to crowdsource innovation, then anybody can be a developer."

If members of your current workforce want to develop their own applications, just imagine how innovative the next generation will be. "We are seeing an emerging workforce of self-helpers," says Jim Fowler, CIO of GE. "Regardless of their discipline, college graduates are coming into our companies and creating models, spreadsheets, and even advanced analytical tools. They come in with the assumption that they don't need an IT organization—they can figure out how to digitize their work themselves. How do CIOs stay relevant in this world of self-helpers? They need to provide the right platforms and guardrails to these workers. They need to be seen as a catalyst and not a speed bump."

Opening the floodgates on innovation is one benefit to treating end users as an extension of the IT organization. Matt Speare, CIO of Regions Bank, has experienced another benefit. "Business unit IT has given our technologists better insight into the drivers of our business," he says. "It has also allowed business unit management to see how complex and interdependent technology actually is." In many companies, end users tend to wonder why IT takes forever. "In managing their own technology, business leaders can see how one little piece of data has to take inputs from eight different upstream systems and feed seven downstream systems," says Spear. "Their knowledge of that interdependency makes them better partners to IT."

Be a Business Team

Once you've stopped battling your business partners over shadow IT, you are ready to develop a less operational, more strategic set of IT resources. In other words, you are ready to transform your team from a technical team into a business team.

As I mentioned in chapter 7, rotational programs are one of the most effective ways to get your technologists to start about the business. At Vanguard, high-potential employees regularly rotate around the company. "Years ago, we rotated an IT leader out of IT to run our very complex institutional operations group," says John Marcante, CIO. "Because that group had some very big people management challenges, the role presented him with a new leadership challenge."

A decade later, Marcante brought this leader back to IT to run Vanguard's data centers. "With DevOps and cloud computing, we were becoming a broker of data center services, rather than just providing compute and storage power," says Marcante. "That strategy required big changes on the people side, and this leader would be well equipped to manage them."

In the absence of (or in addition to) rotational programs, some CIOs are baking business concepts and goals into everything that their teams do. To focus his team on the importance of business goals, Dan Olley, EVP of product development and CTO of Elsevier, makes business goals a part of every conversation and every review. "Everything we do leads with commercial impact," says Olley.

Olley has gone so far as to ban one standard question from steering committee meetings: Are we on time and on budget? To Olley, timescales and budgets are important, but only in the context of whether the project will have commercial benefit. If overruns on budget and time do not affect the commercial benefit, he reasons, should we spend time and money trying to pull them back in? "The response has to be proportionate to the impact on the benefits," he says. "If all you ask about is cost and timeline, then every project that has a hiccup is treated with equal fervor."

When Gerri Martin-Flickinger was CIO of Adobe Systems, she transformed her team from an IT team to a business team by restructuring the organization on a services model. Services fell into three families: employee, business, and technical. Each family was broken into discrete services, including collaboration services, billing services, and storage. "I told my team that they needed to act like the CEO of their service," says Martin-Flickinger. "I want you to know your customers and understand that you'll be out of business if your customers don't buy from you. You are not a utility person; you are the CEO of a small start-up company, and you need to delight your customer all the time."

Martin-Flickinger found that the services structure and the CEO concept helped turn her team into a business team. "Suddenly people started to act like business leaders," she says.

Be the Market

Several months ago, Jeff Donaldson and his team at GameStop deployed iPads, complete with a full suite of customer relationship management functionality, to all of their stores. In developing the apps, they did not go to GameStop's marketing and store operations leaders and ask, "What do you want in a mobile solution?"

Instead, they established their own perspective about how retail companies can drive value with in-store mobile solutions. "We regularly collaborate with industry leaders, and we read success stories about CRM in-store capabilities," says Donaldson. "We delivered the iPad app in our test markets before rolling it out to all of our stores." From their connections to the industry and from their own test markets, the IT team developed a solid point of view about which features will be most important to the retail gaming company's employees and customers.

In the new era of IT, "CIOs have to build capabilities to assess the external marketplace," says Donaldson. "You need to be able to say, 'Given the realities of the external marketplace, we believe that your function should go in this direction.' We have the external perspective to back up that belief. That's a very different role for the CIO."

Be the Revenue

Reframing shadow IT as end-user innovation is one path to being the business. Developing knowledge of the external marketplace is another. But there is nothing so powerful in reconceptualizing IT as placing it directly in your company's revenue stream.

Five years ago, David Anderson became CIO of CH2M Hill, a $6 billion engineering and construction firm. Though he had a strong team, it existed in a culture that he described as "tribal IT"—an IT organization where "several teams and key individuals had significantly more control and authority than they should, and where the overall group was internally focused on keeping the infrastructure and applications running, not on leveraging technology to enable the business," Anderson says.[2]

He also found that IT was consistently in reactive mode: after the company had won a bid for a major new project (like the Panama Canal expansion, or the new Doha Expressway in Qatar), project managers would come to IT and ask for its support. "Then, we'd have to find someone in IT who had specific project management, infrastructure, and applications experience, and send that individual onsite with the project team for an undetermined period of time," says Anderson. "We were reacting, rather than being strategic, and we had to deal with the disruption of carving out one of our people to dedicate to the project."

But Anderson had a plan to form a new group to help the company get out of a reactionary mode.

Building a Business Alliance Group

Anderson built what he calls a "business alliance group," a team of six senior people who are engaged with bid teams before, during, and after major proposals are submitted. "The team is made up of very senior people who have been around IT, the industry, and this company for a long time," says Anderson. "They engage the business early, contribute to the proposal process, and have the time and insight to structure the IT project support team appropriately."

CH2M Hill has ten primary lines of business spanning water, power, energy, environmental, government, transportation, and more. Each person in the business alliance group is dedicated to one or two of the businesses from proposal through to delivery. "Five members of the team were already in IT when we formed the group," says Anderson. "We pulled the sixth from one of our businesses."

Members of the group have visibility into each of the major opportunities coming into the sales pipeline (through the company's CRM system). "We scan and review the pipeline," says Anderson. "What are the long-term programs going to be? Which projects are likely to require a heavy IT element? What are the business opportunities with the highest potential risk?" With detailed knowledge about each new opportunity, members of the business alliance group then engage in the bid process—from proposal preparation to client bid review meetings. As a result, these IT leaders became official members of the "red team," which is essentially a dream team put together to secure the new business.

Upon contract award, the business alliance group selects one member of the IT team to work on the project, typically from one to six months, and then engages with the client and business project owners to provide IT resources to support the project until it is complete.

Reaping the Benefits

One of the true benefits of the business alliance group is that it allows IT costs and processes to be built into the project from the beginning. "Before we set up the group, the project team would come to IT after the contract was awarded," says Anderson. "Often times, the project team had not incorporated all of the IT components into the bid package: hardware, networking, software and applications, security, backups, and the ongoing IT labor costs. By getting out in front of the contract, everyone now understands the project's true business requirements, budget, timeline, and margin potential."

Another, but no less significant, benefit is that by having the business alliance group, Anderson can move the overall discussion of IT from cost to value. "When we put this group together, it began as an overhead cost," says Anderson. "We had to justify every resource. Now, once the team is working on a project, IT participants typically become invaluable, billable resources." By turning the IT group into project-focused and accountable resources, Anderson's team contributes to the overall success and revenue of the project, which affords them the credibility and positioning to raise the perception of IT across the enterprise. Through the business alliance group, Anderson has embedded IT squarely in the business.

Be More Than IT

Perception is a pesky thing. It forms very easily but takes great effort to change. CIOs who spend the first year or so of their tenure on the plumbing side of IT, fixing broken infrastructure in desperate need of attention, can suffer from a techie or operational image that is hard to shake. That "back office" image can create a significant barrier to IT's becoming the business. Those CIOs would do well to journey outside of IT and play highly visible leadership roles that have very little to do with IT operations.

A year after Cora Carmody became CIO of Jacobs Engineering, the $12 billion engineering and construction firm, her CEO asked her to do something new: lead due diligence on the company's next big acquisition.

New to M&A, Carmody was a little apprehensive about the challenge. "I was scared to death, and for a few days, I hoped that they would decide not to do the deal," she says. But her confidence quickly kicked in, and Carmody dove into the job.

As CIO, you have enough on your plate as it is, and with every acquisition, you have the additional responsibility of integrating the technology. Why take on a leadership role at the front end as well? Carmody, who left Jacobs Engineering late in 2015, had two main reasons:

• **Gaining greater knowledge of the business.** "First, we got a prospectus, and determined if the risk and cultural fit made the company worthy of pursuing," says Carmody. "Then we put together an indication of interest, worked with the lawyers, took a small team, and met with the prospective company, and if all went well, we would do real due diligence," she says. "Eventually, we got to a price and a 'go/no-go' decision that we took to the CEO and the board of directors."[3]

All of this work has allowed Carmody to learn a great deal about how to value companies and judge risk. "I could put together a strategic rationale for why a company would be a good acquisition," she says. "That kind of insight was not available to me as CIO."

Carmody also improved her communication skills through her M&A leadership role. "The due diligence report had to be concise, compelling, and complete," she says. "Leading our acquisitions has made me a much better writer, which comes in handy as a CIO."

• **Becoming a better CIO.** Carmody says that, as a result of leading acquisitions for Jacobs Engineering, she has a stronger and broader skillset. "This experience allowed me to build credibility with my business peers in new ways," she says. They began to understand that I am a business leader, not just a techie. They learned that the CIO isn't someone who just pushes gadgets."

If you are ready to follow Carmody's lead and run M&A for a few of your company's next acquisitions, the first step is to make sure your IT organization is in order. The second is to ask for the job. At Jacobs Engineering, the culture is to give additional roles and responsibilities to members of the executive committee. If that is not the culture in your own company, you need to put the bug in your CEO's ear. "You would be surprised by how many CIOs sell themselves short," says Carmody. "If you can raise your hand and make a good case for yourself, it will be worth it. You will be amazed at how much you learn."

Conclusion

For years, we talking heads in the CIO world have been telling CIOs to "know," "partner with," and "build relationships with" the business. While those behaviors will always be important, they are no longer enough.

When IT permeates everything a company does, IT teams can no longer get close to the business; they have to eradicate the distinction between what they do and what the company does. But developing this new business identity in IT takes a lot more work than talking about it. It requires massive changes in organizational structure, skill-sets, and in the hearts and minds of every single employee in the company.

Shadow IT, in reality, is just a nuisance. It's a pain to find yourself responsible for applications you did not build. Much more important than the operational challenge that shadow IT provides is its metaphorical significance. When we reframe shadow IT as end-user innovation, we encourage the business to be IT. When we rotate our people into business areas and back to IT, we blur the lines between technology and business skills. When we organize IT around business services and instruct our people to be the CEO of their services, we encourage IT to be the business, and when, as CIOs, we raise our hands for non-IT leadership roles, we are modeling the way.

Chapter 9

Think Product

When Rob Lux, CIO of Freddie Mac, was in high school, he was in a computer club in which members built computers. One day, a man from Microsoft, which was known at the time for DOS and BASIC, paid the club a visit. "This guy from Microsoft comes out to our little computer club and talks about this new product they're going to be delivering called Windows," says Lux. "He's all excited about it and shows us a demo, and it was horrible."

The demo had only three colors and used tiled windows that couldn't overlap, and when compared with the Mac, which "had just come out and was beautiful," Lux did not think this new Windows product stood a chance.

After the meeting, Lux approached the visitor and said, "You guys are really good at DOS and BASIC. That's your core competency. But in terms of this product, I would hold off. This Windows idea needs a lot of work before it's ready for the market."

The visitor looked Lux square in the eye and said, "I think you're wrong. We're going to push this out now, do frequent revisions, and with hardware getting more powerful, I guarantee you that Windows will be a success."

Many years later, Lux e-mailed the man who had visited his computer club, Bill Gates, and said, "You were right and I was wrong."

"I told the person who would become the richest man in the world, and who made all of his money shipping software, not to ship the most important and successful software product of all time," says Lux, who now has the demo disk, later signed by Gates, hanging on his office wall. Next to the disk, Lux has written: "Ship product early and often," to remind his team to think like a product company.

"When I started at Freddie Mac, it took us eighteen months to get a new software product into people's hands," Lux says. "Now, 80 percent of our software ships in six months or less and 50 percent ships in three months or less. But even that's not fast enough, so we have plans to enhance delivery speed. If you are in the business of technology, ship software," says Lux. "For Bill Gates, it was not about being perfect and having every feature in the product in every release. If you have bugs, communicate them, but ship software, because if you are not getting software into your users' hands, you're failing."

When software is your core business, and shipping it is the only way you make any money, you have a pretty strong driver to ship early and often. But in companies that are not traditional software companies, CIOs have to be that driver themselves. In the new era of IT, when software is becoming a much more integral part of products and services in every industry, CIOs need to work consciously to get their IT organizations to "think product."

Tearing Down the Walls

One major challenge to moving IT toward a product mindset is the long-held division between operations, development, and delivery. "That division creates a project management culture, where the business throws IT a project, and they finish the implementation, but nobody really owns the product end-to-end," says Eash Sundaram, EVP of innovation and CIO of Jet Blue.

Sundaram spent eighteen months reorganizing IT into a product management structure in which a product owner is accountable for the customer or employee experience, regardless of what stage the product is in.

"A product could be a mobile app or our Citrix environment," says Sundaram. "We have one product owner and, within each product, we have plan, build, and operate functions. People who are planning think ahead three to five years about how the product will change. The build people think ahead one to two years, and the operate people think about capacity and reliability now and in the future."

The first step in converting to a product-oriented operating model is removing those long-held silos within IT. "We look at infrastructure, applications, and data holistically, because these three do not exist in isolation," says Sundaram. "They all exist together to deliver an experience. This is the new way my team has to think."

"In IT, we have a product manager for investor experience," says Victor Fetter, CIO of LPL Financial, which provides an integrated platform of brokerage and investment advisor services to more than 14,000 financial advisors. "This person has responsibility for the business analysts, engineers, and the program office; this person is the glue that stitches together the business teams that give input about improving the product. The product manager looks at what it takes to bring something to pilot, what functionality the minimal viable product should contain, and how to expand and support the product over time. The role gets everyone harmonized around how to take this idea from concept all the way to market."

Sundaram and Fetter use the product management function to break down traditional silos within IT, and encourage their teams to think less about their piece of the product, and more comprehensively about the product that the entire team is delivering.

But silos within IT are only some of the traditional structures that must come down in the march toward a product mindset. The walls between IT, product, and marketing must fall as well.

"Every company is becoming a software company, because the products that people are using have some element of software in them," says Jim DuBois, CIO of Microsoft. "This makes the integration between IT and the product organization much more important for disruptive breakthroughs; there is very little that IT or product can do alone."

In any company, the blurring lines between IT and product can create friction, because neither organization wants to relax its faithfulness to its own way of developing software. But with the promise of innovation, better products, and happier customers, it is critical to blur the lines, which requires conscious change on the part of the CIO. "We need to change our language and our processes," says Jim DuBois, CIO of Microsoft. "IT and product have to get more similar in how we use Agile and DevOps and how we think about processes like incident management."

Dubois keeps his eye out for places where multiple teams are working on different dimensions of the same product and puts those people together. "Let's put them all on the same team," he says. "I don't care whether that team reports to me in IT or to the product organization, but let's not have two teams working on the same thing. Let's make it one team to take the friction out. Rearranging teams for focus is a powerful tool we can use to accelerate the right value."

Putting IT into the Product

When Gerri Martin-Flickinger was CIO at Adobe, she and her team removed the barriers between IT and product by having IT deliver value directly into the Adobe product line. They started by moving

Adobe's back-office functions to a services-oriented architecture because, "You have to make that back office sing before you move closer to the product," she says.

Adobe IT had been running fifteen different approval systems, which created a great deal of complexity for the company's employees. "We wanted to present a unified experience for our employees, whether they were working on travel and expense, recruiting, or purchasing approvals."

So, Martin-Flickinger and her team built an SOA model that provided a buffer between employees and a large number of back-office and SaaS solutions. The simple user interface was delivered across platforms, so employees could do a range of approvals from their mobile devices in one interface with a simple click. Taking this approach allowed the IT department to modernize their back-office systems while not disrupting the user community. "Employees loved the interface for its ease of use," says Martin-Flickinger. "IT loved it because it gave them increased architectural freedom."

Having built a single successful SOA-based solution for Adobe's back-office functions, Martin-Flickinger and her team saw that they could do more. They could build a services layer that could be used right inside the Adobe product.

"Traditionally, Adobe's product engineers have been responsible for any functionality that went into the product," Martin-Flickinger says. "But today, Adobe's IT organization is providing a services gateway that handles all e-commerce transactions across Adobe Creative Cloud products and services."

When customers enter Adobe's Creative Cloud, everything they see on the screen was developed by the Adobe product engineering team. When they get to the point where they enter their credit-card information to buy the product, the user experience is no different than if the e-commerce functionality was embedded right in the product. "But it's not," says Martin-Flickinger. "It's actually being delivered by a web service that's run by IT. We put IT-offered services right into the product."

With IT providing this functionality to the Adobe product, product engineers had more time to focus on new customer-facing features "It was a win-win-win," says Martin-Flickinger. "IT engineers were providing functionality that helped product engineers deliver products to market faster, which made our customers happy."

One key learning for Martin-Flickinger was that product engineers are skeptical of IT until IT proves they can work hand-in-hand with them. "Find one really smart engineering type in your IT organization and put them on a skunk-works project with one product engineer," she advises. "You need to identify an IT person who looks and smells like a product engineer; it needs to be someone the engineering people like." If you do this right, says Martin-Flickinger, that person will become your ambassador. "That way, when someone in engineering says, 'What do you think of involving IT in this?' the engineering team will be supportive."

By breaking down traditional lines between IT and product, Martin-Flickinger was able to leverage her relationship with Adobe's product and marketing leaders into a new and powerful data capability for the company. "Data insight is a three-legged stool of back-office, behavioral, and product data," she says. "Combining what happens at the point of your product with your back-office and behavioral data is incredibly powerful. That's where you get the real insights. It means reinventing those three spheres of data, whether you're selling software, dishwashers, or cars."

But in most organizations, the three legs of the data stool are owned by three different departments, each with different skill-sets and cultures. It is very hard to get product and IT engineers to participate in a single, integrated data model, because they are all extremely smart and committed to their own approaches. How do you corral them into following one architectural standard?

"With behavioral data, the biggest challenge is the traditional relationship between marketing and IT," says Martin-Flickinger. "Both sides have to let go of historical boundaries, because historical boundaries won't work in this model."

Martin-Flickinger suggests you plow ahead through the cultural differences and get your best engineers to create some kind of unified data model, and not worry about getting it right. "At some point, you have to get your data stitched together," she says. "The model may not be right the first time, but if you don't get it unified, you're never going to get started." Expect this to be difficult, says Martin-Flickinger, because people may lose access to the databases they have come to rely on. "That's pretty emotional for people," she says.

With the back-office IT team, your work is what it always is: getting IT to care about the impact of the data and the business goals the data is serving, not just the technical task at hand. "Your IT people have to understand the business needs that the data stitching is driving," says Martin-Flickinger. "The people who were good at building really big data models ten years ago are probably not the right people for this next phase. Your people need to understand why one piece of data is important to the business and why another is not. That's a different kind of thinker."

For CIOs who have stepped into the digital leadership void (see chapter 1) and are leading their company's digital strategy, thinking product is a necessity. "Product management is different in digital than in IT," says Donagh Herlihy, EVP of digital and CIO at Bloomin' Brands. "In IT, your business partners define their requirements. In digital, you don't have that luxury; you define requirements yourself based on deep consumer insight." This means making decisions with imperfect information, and learning from your customers' response to your solutions. "You need to surround yourself with product managers and strong digital analytics people, so your solutions are grounded in consumer needs," Herlihy says. "This way, when you put new solutions out there, you can quickly read how consumers are responding to them."

Six Steps to Product Innovation

As EVP of product development and CTO of Elsevier, Dan Olley is responsible for the traditional IT functions of infrastructure and business automation. But, that only represents about 30 percent of what his technology organization does. The rest is focused on software product development. "With an ever-increasing percentage of Elsevier's revenue coming from online products, we have had to reinvent ourselves to compete with the world's best product technology companies," Olley says.

How does an IT organization that finds itself responsible for product innovation reinvent itself to become a world-class technology division? That's what I asked Olley, who has boiled it down into six steps:

• **Step one: Know the problem and how you'll measure success.** "It's amazing how many times people say, 'We're going to build this great new solution,' but when you ask them what problem they're trying to solve and for whom, they are not always quite so clear," says Olley. Defining a product or feature by the problem it's going to solve for a defined group is the key. "We bring customers, and potential customers, into our ideation lab and test ideas with them before we build anything. We work with them to define the real-life problems they're experiencing and how we can help solve them. When we truly understand what success looks like for our current and potential customers before we start, we can build products that deliver tangible value. This is something you can't do in a vacuum; you have to get your customers involved."

- **Step two: Talk to noncustomers.** When organizations are expanding, extending, or upgrading existing products, they always talk to existing customers, but this is not enough, says Olley. "Many of our online products started life as new incarnations of more traditional offline products. Existing customers tend to tell you how you can improve what you currently do. This is important, but innovation often comes when you ask the people who should be customers, who have the problem you are setting out to solve, why they aren't customers today. Existing customers give you enhancements; noncustomers provide you with whole new areas of functionality."

- **Step three: Prototype with your existing and potential users.** Once you can articulate the problem and how you'll measure success, "build early, build quick, and play it back," says Olley. "We do lightweight wire-framing long before we start full-scale development. We need to know if we have it right before we get started."

- **Step four: Go live with a minimum viable product.** "Your first version should be a minimum viable product, the least functional version that you can deliver while still solving the problem," says Olley. "Your users will tell you very quickly what's wrong with the solution and what else you need. If you build something bigger than a minimal viable product, you could be adding functionality that your users don't need."

- **Step five: Deliver through small, multidisciplined teams.** "Throwing projects from one group to another will not cut it when you are innovating with revenue generating products," Olley says. He co-locates developers, UX experts, architects, and selected customers into a small team with a common understanding of the problem, the vision, and the commitment to deliver as one unit.

• **Step six: Do some reconnaissance.** Olley has an advanced technology team that is out in front of the product development groups, evaluating new technologies well before the development team is ready to apply them to a new product. "We are breaking in new technologies before we need them," Olley says. "When our product groups are prototyping a solution, we have already evaluated, in a general sense, the set of technologies they will use."

Conclusion

How do you take IT professionals who for decades have been measured on their ability to manage their own piece of an implementation and get them to think about the bigger picture? How do you wipe away years of distrust between two functions, IT and marketing, and get them to work together on teams and to integrate back-office and front-office data? When your business no longer merely runs on software but, in one way or another, drives revenue from software, how do IT and the product organization begin to work as one?

As usual, it all starts with the CIO. Yes, the CIO has to hire product managers and work through team conflict and introduce Agile, DevOps, and all the rest of it. But before any of that, the CIO has to do something counterintuitive to a position with so much operational responsibility: let go of your own need for organizational boundaries. "Sometimes I'm moving IT people into the product organization," says Jim Dubois. "But I'm still held accountable, at the company level, for the work that those teams do. I can no longer care about who reports to product and who reports to me. I have to feel as accountable for the outcomes, regardless of where the work happens. That's a new mindset for the CIO."

As CIO, you spend all day every day changing the hearts and minds of your staff, your business partners, and the executive committee. Their perspectives on accountability, boundaries, and roles are deep and the outcome of a bygone industrial economy in which lines were solid and empires were important. In the digital economy, boundaries are permeable, big organizations are a liability, and we can no longer be clear about exactly where IT stops and product starts. This means that CIOs need to rethink their own biases about ownership before asking their teams to do the same.

Chapter 10

Go Faster

As an executive recruiter who specializes in IT leadership, I spend a lot of time with CEOs who tell me what they want from their new CIO. "IT is not fast enough," they often say. "We sign big checks and launch big projects, but the return on those investments comes way too late, if at all. We need our CIO to deliver faster."

It always surprises me, then, that when I ask CIOs about what prevents their IT teams from moving more quickly, they talk as much about corporate culture as they do their IT organizations. Sure, IT could develop and deliver more quickly, but IT's business partners have to change their habit of waiting around for solutions.

For the last twenty years, IT has developed and delivered technology solutions the same way: CIOs and their teams met with their business partners, wrote down the "business requirements order," developed a set of technical specifications, took nine months (or even two years) to build the solution, and then showed up with their fingers crossed that the final product would fulfill that original set of requirements. But, while business leaders gripe about this Waterfall development process, they are not always eager to spend the time and resources on a more iterative development cycle.

"Our business partners are used to requesting high-end solutions, and we're talking to them about minimal viable product," says Victor Fetter, CIO of LPL Financial. "It can seem like a disconnect for them when we start with a small solution, gain insights, and evolve from there. It takes changing the culture to one that buys into a process just as much as an end product. That calls for a new way of thinking for many executive teams; it's the CIO's job to change the culture and set expectations for the new development process."

Julia Anderson, CIO of Smithfield Foods, and her team are currently working on a large systems implementation to support a major consolidation and transformation of their U.S. businesses. "One of the first things we did was build a standard prototype and use it as a basis for conversations with key business and functional leaders," she says. "How would you use this tool? What features don't we need? We didn't do any requirements definition at all; we built the prototype, got input, and now we're building the solution. This took a lot of time out of the development and delivery process."

While the executive team may cling to the old development model, the newest generation of end users cannot stomach it at all. "We used to put in one big ERP that would define every process," says Ralph Loura, CTO of Rodan + Fields. "But the 'one big monolithic way to do everything' doesn't fly with millennials. They want the freedom to create changes much more easily. This means that IT needs to work with much smaller components—microservices—that are loosely coupled. This way, as long as you adhere to a rigid API, you can change almost everything you want inside the container."

Call it microservices, Agile, minimal viable product, iterative development, or whatever you like, the new SDLC is a major departure for everyone in your company. It requires a huge perspective shift for your team, your workforce, and your business partners.

As anyone who has moved to an iterative development model will tell you, it takes two to be Agile. If IT's relationship with the rest of the business is poor, there is no Agile program in the world that will help you. If you have a strong enough relationship with your business partners to introduce Agile, then an iterative approach to development will strengthen that relationship even more. "Agile will not do any good for your organization if you don't have product owners on the business side willing and empowered to make big decisions about tradeoffs in the moment," says Vanguard's John Marcante. "So as CIO, you spend a lot of time making sure that the business understands their role in an Agile methodology."

In deciding where to start, Mandy Edwards, former CIO of CBRE, suggests you find a business partner who is struggling with a long-term plan. "In some cases you can use an iterative approach when a business partner doesn't necessarily know the longer term outcome of what he or she is trying to achieve," she says. "By using a fail-fast, continuous learning approach to deployment, that executive could learn enough to build out a longer-term strategy. That is the person to start with."

But while you are identifying the one or two key partners to get your iterative program off the ground, you'll also need to be thinking about the broader culture of your company.

"When it comes to adopting a nimble 'test and learn' mindset, the largest obstacle for big companies is culture," says Marcante. "The company now has to value a continuous cycle of hypothesis, testing, failing, and learning. This means establishing a culture where 'failure' is not a bad word. That is a new way to think, and large companies are trying to figure out how to get there."

When working with his executive peers on concepts like "fast failure," Marcante looks to Eric Ries's book *The Lean Startup,* which provides large companies with lessons learned from Silicon Valley startups.

"This 'test and learn' approach that Ries describes has caught on like wildfire at Vanguard," Marcante says. "In fact, our head of product development is applying the Lean Startup approach to R&D. I can rattle off a ton of IT initiatives where we are applying those lessons, but when you see those concepts take off in product R&D, you know you've really hit on something."

OK. You've identified a few key executives ripe for an iterative SDLC, and believe it or not, you've gotten your entire company to begin to understand that "smart failure" is not an oxymoron. You would think that changing the culture of the IT organization, which is under your direct control, would be the easiest part of an Agile transformation. But it is often the toughest.

Most IT people take their jobs very seriously, and for the last several decades, their jobs demanded control. If you can't touch it, you can't manage it. If you outsource it, you lose control. If the business controls their own IT resources, we introduce risk into the enterprise, and so on....

The need for control can be so deep and intractable in your own IT people that it can impede your ability to make an iterative SDLC framework successful. Uprooting this mindset can often require a major overhaul of your entire organizational design.

Teams of Teams

To deliver faster at GE, CIO Jim Fowler has flattened his IT organization into a "teams of teams" structure in which co-located groups own a small, minimal viable product deliverable that they can produce in ninety days. The team focuses on one piece of work that they will own through its complete life cycle.

"In the old world, you might have run an ERP application where people from a server team understood the compute infrastructure that it ran on," Fowler says. "People from a networking team understood the networking components that were hooked up to those machines.

People on another team ran the database elements. And then you probably had yet another team doing interface architecture for how that ERP talked to other applications. And each of those teams was independent from the other so that when you had a production problem, you had this 'he said, she said' phenomenon, and you had to get seven different people from different teams on the phone to figure out the problem; it took forever."

In a teams-of-teams world, the team includes a database administrator, a network administrator, an infrastructure person, and a developer. "They work together every day to make sure that ERP delivers the outcome that our end users need," Fowler says. "The teams of teams breaks down those silos."

Fowler is also investing heavily in retraining his workforce for this new era. "I've got people who are still writing deep code in COBOL," he says. "That is not the agile workforce that I need for the future," he says. "One of the ways we are retraining is by replatforming most of our applications to run in the cloud. We are doing that through ninja teams—ten people from different areas of technology who leave their day job to go to our West Coast technology center and spend three weeks porting one application to run in the cloud."

The teams train with GE's West Coast developers, and when they return, they own the replatformed application. "This year, we'll retrain over six hundred workers through that process," says Fowler. "That's how I'm driving an agile mentality that values technology ownership."

Fowler is also driving faster delivery by changing the sourcing model in IT. "Today, I have five thousand IT professionals who work for GE and fourteen thousand contractors. Those fourteen thousand contractors are great people, but they are just not as invested in the success of the company as the five thousand employees," he says. "So, to ignite the workforce, I am insourcing. Over the next two years, I will hire two thousand people into one of five global technology centers around the world, which are organized by the teams-of-teams mentality. We are bringing the knowledge content, intellectual property, and the real know-how back inside the company."

Fowler is not the first to recognize the adverse impact that outsourced workforces can have on speed of delivery. When Dave Smoley became CIO of AstraZeneca, the sourcing model was "a complex ecosystem of multiple third-party suppliers who were involved in everything we did," he says. "We had multiple handoffs, so you had to get ten people in a room to make a change." Smoley reduced his outsourced services from 70 percent of his portfolio to 30 percent, and has minimized the handoffs, which has enabled the team to move faster.

Five Steps to Building Urgency in IT

Whether you are moving to a more iterative development framework or not, your team needs to approach their work with much more urgency than they have in the past. As usual, it all starts with you.

As a CIO, you can only push a handful of messages out to your team consistently. For Steve Zerby, CIO of Owens Corning, the $5 billion building materials maker, one of those messages is "urgency."

"When you are in a service business like IT, you need to act with as much urgency—or more—than those you are providing service to," Zerby says. "The positive feeling you want to create is predicated on your organization's demonstration that your business partners' challenges are as important to you as they are to them. When they feel like their hair is on fire and you act like it isn't a big deal, everyone loses."[1]

Urgency, to Zerby, is not an emotion; it is a culture. "As CIO, you have to talk about urgency," he says, "but it is more important to create an environment where urgency happens naturally." He sees this process as having five steps:

- **Step one: Put leaders in the right position.** At Owens Corning, Zerby co-locate many of his senior leaders with the businesses they support. "The first step toward creating a culture of urgency is to put your senior leaders in a position—which includes their physical environment—where they can build relationships with their counterparts," he says. "They need to be present in the meetings where strategies are made, and it needs to be natural that they are included in those meetings."

- **Step two: Give leaders broad latitude.** "If a business leader is confronted with an urgent situation, and the IT leader says, 'I have to check with someone, because that's not my responsibility,' it's like seeing someone drowning in a swimming pool, and saying, 'I could save you, but I'm not the lifeguard,'" says Zerby. "As CIO, you need to give your people the authority to make a broad set of decisions in real time."

- **Step three: Pick the right leaders.** "The senior leaders I position with our business partners each have twenty years of experience across different realms of IT, and some are in their second career," says Zerby. "There are few urgent situations that come up that they haven't seen before. They are able to rely on a lifetime of experience and good judgment."

- **Step four: Provide leaders with adequate resources.** It is one thing to demonstrate urgency and another to get something done. "Latitude and positioning without resources won't get you far," says Zerby. "Our senior IT business leaders have a small, lean team that is dynamic and athletic enough that they can get 80 percent of issues resolved right away without going anywhere else." Zerby places more importance on leaders with a broad set of skills than on specialists. "When it comes to acting with urgency, it is more important for our team to be wide than deep," he says.

- **Step five: Establish clear principles.** To establish a culture of urgency, you need to be clear about the principles by which your IT organization operates, says Zerby. "If you don't want your leaders stopping by your office after every meeting to make sure they make the right decision, put your fundamental principles on paper so that your team can understand them," he says. "When we built our leadership team, we told them, 'If you are in a situation and can provide immediate action to resolve it, my expectation is that you are going to do it whether you are formally responsible for it or not.'"

When Speed Is Nonnegotiable

Sometimes, the best way to build speed into your IT organization is to commit to a nearly impossible but nonnegotiable deadline. In August 2012, SAIC, the $11 billion national security, engineering, and enterprise IT provider, announced that it would split in two: SAIC would deliver enterprise IT services to the government sector, and a new company, Leidos, would provide services in security, health, and engineering.

This meant that the SAIC IT team had twelve months to stand up infrastructures for both companies, under a program they called "Gemini." The existing infrastructure was complex: it ran more than three hundred applications, two enterprise private cloud data centers, 1,660 servers, had three hundred terabytes of storage, and supported thirty-two thousand end-user computers. Spinning two infrastructures out of this one—in only twelve months—would not be an easy task.

"The cutover went precisely as planned," says Bob Logan, who was CIO of SAIC at the time. "All major tasks were executed, all systems went live on schedule, and there were no surprises." The team achieved this feat of strength by following three basic principles:[2]

- **Let's see what this cloud can do.** "We had just spent eighteen months building and then migrating to our new enterprise private cloud data centers," says Logan. "The infrastructure was designed to be scalable from a compute and storage perspective, as well as having a robust and flexible security architecture."

Two months after SAIC had migrated to the enterprise private cloud, the company announced the separation. "The IT team knew they had a modern data center built to best practices," says Logan. "They also had a deep understanding of what was running in it, having just touched every system during the migration process." This very deep and current knowledge gave the team the confidence to stand up the two infrastructures in such a short time.

- **Clone everything.** Both of the new companies had to continue to meet a significant number of compliance and regulatory requirements. "This meant that we had to ensure that the data, systems, and processes which ran both companies on day one of separation would be accurate copies of their approved sources," says Logan. "We had to ensure auditable rigor on all cloning, replicating, and duplicating processes."

- **One team, one goal.** The Gemini program included the implementation, before formal separation, of organizational and other changes that would prepare both new companies for what their world would be like after separation. As senior management began to make those changes, Logan decided that the IT team would remain as one during Gemini, regardless of where team members would wind up after the separation.

Before he began, Logan had identified these three principles as critical to the success of the Gemini program. Looking back now, however, he saw additional elements that led to Gemini's success:

- **Tight timeline.** Because Logan and his team had such a crisp and well-defined due date, there was no room for second guessing decisions or wasting time. "Because of the deadline, I saw very purposeful decision making," says Logan. "We were focused on prioritization, almost minute by minute, because we were heading for that single goal. This required a level of cooperation that I have not seen before in my experience as CIO."

- **Eyes on the horizon.** "My job was always to look to the next horizon," says Logan, "which was very hard to do with so much happening every day. I needed always to be looking one or two hills ahead to clear those obstacles that might slow us down."

Logan cites as an example the amount of time it took SAIC's leadership team to decide on a name for the company. For a number of legal reasons, choosing a name took a while. "But, at a technology level, we needed that name," Logan says. "The name is at the heart of our active directory. The name feeds into our security systems, and our servers. The name feeds into our authentication systems. The name is embedded into our workflow."

The IT team came up with creative ways to cordon off and do as much as they could without the name, but "the IT team was a horse in the Kentucky Derby," says Logan. "We were in the gate and ready to go." As the team was working around the naming obstacle, Logan's role was to "take a geeky detail and elevate it to the executive committee," he says. "I told them that I might just call the new company 'Bob'!"

Tradition has it that crew members of a newly commissioned ship in the Navy earn the moniker "plankowner." Logan believes this an apt metaphor for his IT team. "My team and I went through the crucible and we are leaner and more agile as a result," says Logan. "Gemini presented us with an accelerated learning curve, where we touched every piece of the infrastructure. We are all plankowners now, and you can't put a price on that."

Six Principles for PayPal's IT Spinoff

Brad Strock, CIO of PayPal, also faced a situation in which speed was nonnegotiable. In September of 2014, eBay announced plans to spin off its PayPal subsidiary as an independent, publicly traded company. Within a few weeks of the announcement, PayPal's technology leaders had nine months to separate from eBay and set up the infrastructure and systems to support the new company. (Outside experts predicted a separation timeline of eighteen to twenty-four months, or double the amount of time PayPal's technology groups actually received.)[3]

The new structure would include nine hundred applications, thirty thousand end-user devices, twenty-five thousand e-mail accounts, nineteen hundred vendor contracts, three new data centers, one of the largest enterprise data warehouses in the world, and the addition of five thousand new servers, with the recreation, cloning, or moving of another nine thousand across sixty global locations.

"Everything was in the eBay domain, so we had to build entirely new IT for PayPal without exception," Strock says. "But we had half the time we really needed." To keep the massive IT project on track, he developed six key principles:

- **Clone and go.** "Our rule was to take what was there and split it, because every time you touch something, you are tempted to improve it," Strock says. From time to time, he and his team allowed exceptions to this rule when an upgrade would produce no additional risk. "We took the opportunity of the separation to take Exchange to the cloud with Office 365," he says. "We knew we were going there eventually and that the move would not add risk to the separation."

- **Avoid big bangs.** Strock wanted to avoid the potentially disruptive experience of flipping a switch on the new network and lighting everyone up on one day. "We wanted everything to be iterative, so that we could touch one thousand users a day, rather than all thirty thousand at once."

The plan sounded great from a change management perspective, but it created some real engineering challenges for the IT team. "We had to build a separate corporate network for all of the PayPal employees, who were co-located with eBay staff," Strock says. "That meant we had to let PayPal employees work on the eBay network until the day of the split, and then transfer only those people to the new network." While that complexity made the work harder, it let the IT team track how they were progressing on a daily basis.

- **Be very transparent.** Strock and his team identified a small number of critical outcomes and "tracked them maniacally." For example, they knew that thirty thousand people needed to be migrated to new services. "Every day, we looked at where we were on that journey—five thousand? six thousand? We were always aware of where we were on the flight path to hit our goal." This enabled them to communicate status and progress with clarity and consistency to all major stakeholders.

- **Raise risk issues early.** "Bad news doesn't get better with age," Strock says. "We had to get the teams comfortable with raising risk issues early, when we still had the time to take action." Before the separation project, Strock had always worked hard to instill risk transparency into the IT culture, "but it became much more important during this transformation," he says.

- **Secure "air cover."** Before the team embarked on the separation, Strock sat down with every executive, including the CEO, and briefed him or her on the scope of the work, including the big numbers and the tight timelines. "We wound up scaring them a little bit, and every executive responded with 'how can we help?'" Strock's answer: "There will be bumps in the road and things will break. We just ask for your grace and support while we work through it." This enabled the separation team to work without worrying that, if they made a mistake, there would be major repercussions. "I didn't realize the power of the 'air cover' principle until later," says Strock. "I didn't realize how much freedom it would give our teams to move quickly."

- **Identify single points of accountability.** For every major piece of work, Strock identified one person who would be accountable for the outcome. "When you have multiple people accountable, you don't have anyone accountable," he says. As a corollary to this principle, Strock kept the teams small. "For a small core team, fewer than one hundred people, we took almost everything else off their plates," he says. "This meant few people debating decisions, better focus, and faster progress."

As a result of the separation, Strock now finds himself with a stronger team. "In a merger, you're looking for synergy, but here, you're looking for the opposite," he says. "It was important that we have a strong team to run IT for PayPal, and this project was a battlefield promotion that built our bench strength."

Strock also finds that he is now a stronger leader. "I am an analytical person, but this project required us all just to make decisions and move on," he says. "I had to be candid and call it like it was, and not spend time worrying about politics. It was liberating."

Conclusion

In the olden days, IT would take the time it needed to introduce a new technology to the organization: it would roll out a pilot to a set of users, then to a larger group, and then to the entire organization. Today, with consumerization, technology solutions, one way or another, are already in the hands of users before IT even gets involved. Either users have adopted the technology in their personal lives, or as leaders, they have decided not to wait for IT; they just purchased it themselves.

This means that IT is in catch-up mode all the time. To get ahead of the curve, we all need to move faster. CIOs must position "urgency" as one of their organization's cultural touchstones, eradicate the IT professional's traditional need for control, and treat huge new projects as a workshop in learning to iterate and be faster. But perhaps most importantly, they must remember that, in the new era of IT, "being the business" means involving business leaders in the actual development of technology solutions.

For years, we have allowed our business partners to be naïve consumers of our technology products. They tell us what they need, and we deliver. But this relationship will no longer stand. Just as the IT budget cannot belong to IT alone, and IT should not be solely responsible for driving technology adoption, the development process cannot remain squarely in IT. To deliver faster, we need to trim down the translation process between business need and technology solution. We need to treat our IT people as business people and our business people as technology innovators. The "us and them" divide has to go if we are to meet the tremendous demand and awesome promise of technology in the new era of IT.

Conclusion

A New CIO for a New Era

A few months ago, I was talking with Bruce Hoffmeister, global CIO of Marriott International, about the kinds of skills he was cultivating in IT. He talked about management consulting and how important it was for his team to counsel leaders throughout the global company about how technology can help drive business strategy.

When I asked Clark Golestani, CIO of Merck, the same question, he told me about the critical role that venture capitalists were playing in his IT organization. Kim Stevenson, CIO of Intel, has put a premium on data scientists.

So, let's see: management consultants, VCs, and data scientists—that's quite a range of skill-sets. Of course, we must include information security experts, enterprise architects, Agile developers, project managers, and business relationship executives. Oh, and let's not forget help desk supervisors, communications directors, and systems administrators. Can you think of another business function that requires such a dazzling array of skills?

This growing range of skill-sets that CIOs need in their organizations has led me to an existential consideration: When something becomes everything, is it anything? Or even better: When something becomes everything, what is it?

In the new era of IT, when technology is the business, the way IT organizes itself, manages its supply chain, and integrates with the rest of the company is going through a major conceptual and structural change. This was my learning from the interviews that I conducted for this book, and from the many conversations I've had with CIOs since.

In fact, when I presented some of the concepts in this book to the CIO council at the National Retail Federation earlier this year, Paul Chapman, CIO of Gap Inc., commented that, in his view, the new model for IT was an internal professional services firm that delivers a diverse set of services to the company in which it resides: management consulting, application development, security, end-user support, and innovation, to name only a few.

An internal professional services firm that provides everything from management consulting to help desk support not only requires a range of skills, it also demands that the executive committee understands the central role that IT now plays in the business.

This was the conclusion that Dave Smoley came to when he joined AstraZeneca as CIO in 2013. "In 1990s and early 2000s, people in this company said that we were not an IT company, we were a drug company, and that we should focus on designing and manufacturing drugs, not IT," says Smoley. As part of that early philosophy, the company outsourced a huge number of IT functions, which Smoley has brought back in-house. "IT is the business now," he says. "IT has shifted from being about procurement to being about leadership. That means we need skills in marketing, commercial operations, and sales."

Bruce Hoffmeister is well on his way toward developing IT as the internal professional services firm that Paul Chapman describes. He has a group in IT called "partnership and planning," whose members are often co-located with colleagues from marketing, reservations, or human resources; they become members of those teams. "Their role is to develop a business intimacy with each discipline to understand its goals, challenges, and what motivates its employees," says Hoffmeister. "This group does not walk in talking about the IT plan; they talk about the marketing, finance, or reservations plan and then advise on how we can drive those plans with technology."

The secret sauce of Marriott's partnership and planning group is how tight they are with the architecture and development groups. "The planning group is not simply a marketing function talking to the other disciplines," says Hoffmeister. "We're developing true business leaders who are working with leaders from other areas to advance their cause."

This development of true business leaders in IT is a sticky wicket. The traditional enabling function of IT has been at odds with growing the kinds of professionals who can lead in this new internal professional services firm model. "Our current generation of IT leaders grew up in a world where they never had to take any personal risk," says Scott McKay, CIO of Genworth Financial. "They are well compensated for just managing a queue of tasks and asking people what's important." This cushy, well-paid, low-risk situation has a lot of IT leaders resisting the new strategic role of IT. "It will be another decade before our organizations and educational institutions adopt the view that IT can be a business driver," says McKay. "Until then, CIOs will need to bifurcate their organizations into two: the people who drive change and the people who play out their career in the cost part of the organization."

If your organization is filled with IT professionals who are resistant to a new strategic role, then look elsewhere, suggests Bruce Lee, who became CIO of Fannie Mae in 2014 and is now the company's SVP and head of operations and technology. "Over time, a greater percentage of IT services will be delivered by people from outside of

IT," Lee says. "CIOs have to lift themselves to the enterprise level and realize that IT is just a part of the chain in delivering business value." Lee sees the emergence of chief data officers as a case in point. "You will start to see chief data officers with operational roles," he says. "They will clean and serve data and will pull those functional roles away from application delivery teams. The worst mistake a CIO can make is trying accumulate all of a company's IT skills inside the IT organization."

As IT innovation, investment management, and delivery move to a shared model, so will IT funding. "Instead of funding individual projects, we are going to start seeing companies that fund cross-functional teams that decide on which projects to fund," says Matt Speare, CIO of Regions Bank. "Instead of deciding to spend $8 million on a new system, companies will spend $8 million to fund five teams who work together to determine what the next round of capabilities should be."

If the CIO's role shifts from delivering IT to managing a professional services firm and presiding over a cross-functional team of delivery people, what skills do CIOs need themselves?

As Ralph Loura mentioned toward the beginning of this book, today's CIO must be "the master of almost everything, including technology."

A CIO's technology knowledge comes in handy in the new era of IT because, according to Bruce Lee, CIO of Fannie Mae, the new IT operating model will rely on a new architectural model. Shared services, says Lee, started out at the network layer, but with platforms as a service delivery tool, shared services are moving up the stack.

"We are seeing a fundamental shift in the IT ecosystem where our employees and customers want to create their own functionality," says Lee. "We need to remove the translation layer and allow them to design their own website experience, decide which products they want, and even do self-provisioning in B-to-B spaces."

In this new world, there is no boundary between the business and IT. "Instead, IT provides a set of capabilities, like security, data, and user experience, which people can consume both inside and outside the walls of the company," Lee says.

This means rethinking shared services as a concept: "Most shared services organizations have been created as a cost saver with service catalogs and unit pricing. As a result, shared services have been associated with standards and constraints," says Lee. "Now, shared services, in the form of a services architecture, have to be thought of as enablers moving speed and flexibility to the front of the business and out of the IT department. Those are some significant changes to the traditional IT operating model."

For Dave Smoley, "My new operating model is much more boundaryless. Part of being effective in this new world is not boxing yourself in and defining yourself by how others have traditionally defined you. If you understand social and mobile and you are out there embracing, adopting, and learning about those technologies, then you will lead in marketing, HR, and operations, not only in IT. You cannot let yourself be held back by traditional definitions and boundaries around roles and responsibilities."

Bruce Lee embraced this notion of openness when he joined Fannie Mae as CIO. "Many of my CIO peers create their own governance and build walls around their function in order to protect it and give it an identity," he says. "When I joined Fannie Mae, I took the opposite approach and said that IT is completely open. The fact is, the CIO is managing the largest and most complicated entity in the enterprise. It's this competency of trust, openness, and connecting at all levels that is the distinguishing feature of a successful CIO, because without trust and openness, the job is nearly impossible."

Jim Fowler, CIO of GE, sees three CIO models emerging: two that will enable the CIO to be effective and relevant, and one that will not. There is the back-office CIO, who controls infrastructure, the network, storage, and makes the PCs run. "The CIOs who choose to play that role will not be relevant for long," says Fowler. "People are quickly realizing that they can procure IT services for themselves much more efficiently than CIOs can provide them from a centralized IT organization." Then there is the CIO as operator, where CIOs use their end-to-end understanding of processes to act as chief operating officers, designing the most lean and digital way to run a process. "As digital just becomes the way we work, CIOs will no longer be leaders of an IT function," says Fowler. "They will lead almost all of a company's shared services."

And finally, there is the commercial CIO, who is essentially a "chief technology officer who shows the company's leaders how digital products and services will enhance whatever they made and sold before; they will help to manage digital disruption." To stay relevant in the new era of IT, says Fowler, CIOs need to be operating leaders or commercial leaders or a hybrid of both.

The ability to predict the future has always been critical to the CIO role; today, that skill needs to be even more acute. "Looking into the future and trying to anticipate how technology will change is different and more challenging than in the past," says Mandy Edwards, CIO of CBRE. "In the past we could just go talk to the software provider that we were already investing in. It was relatively easy to know what was going to happen through those top-tier providers." But today, companies are using a much greater breadth of technology providers, so finding a path through that assortment of options has become much more important to the CIO role.

"I laugh because I spent the first part of my career working with three-tiered architecture and taking the database out of the process layer," says Julia Anderson, CIO of Smithfield Foods. "And now here we are again putting all of the databases back online. Everything that goes around comes around. A big part of my job as CIO is to compare what we did in the past with what we will do in the future, and how we can do it better this time."

Oh, how I would love to draw this book into a tidy conclusion. It would be wonderful to provide the be-all, end-all blueprint of the new IT operating model, the new skill-set for CIOs, and the perfect prescription for creating a culture that allows IT to be the business. But from my conversations with CIOs across a wide spectrum of industries and businesses, I do not think we are there yet. We are not ready to define concretely what it means to be a CIO in the new era of IT. We know that CIOs must relinquish their need to control (while still safeguarding the enterprise from all possible threats, of course.) We know that the walls between IT and its business partners must come down. We know that IT has to toggle between the how and the what, and we know that we need to teach our teams to lead.

My approach to writing this book sits squarely in the digital age. I call it "iterative content development," where I have thrown out some concepts to you, my beloved readership, in the form of blogs and newsletters and live presentations. You have been thoughtful and generous in your responses, which I have baked right back into my work. I see this book as a minimal viable product to submit to you, my partners in developing relevant ideas about the role of the CIO. I look forward to learning your thoughts on this product as we continue our long and fruitful dialogue about the future of IT.

And now, in the spirit of iterative content development, I present to you some of my favorite quotes that I have lifted straight from my conversations with all of my CIO friends and tweeted out to you over the last year. Forget the poets, the authors, and the playwrights. Keep your songwriters and your sonneteers. When I crave wit, wisdom, pith, and pathos, I turn to the most eloquent wordsmiths of all—CIOs!

My Favorite CIO Quotes

- You have to make the back office sing before you can move closer to the product.
- Avoid the scenario where there's the digital conversation, and then there's the IT conversation.
- Security will always be the top priority for CIOs, whether they know it or not.
- To drive change, you have to throw your pride out the window.
- It is pointless to have metrics without consequences.
- There is an inverse relationship between the maturity of a vendor and its ability to innovate.
- Every cool thing you do today is a support cost tomorrow.
- It's hard to start in the datacenter and find your way to the user.
- The amount of time between a disruptive idea and massive adoption is shorter than ever.
- Big companies have to start valuing a culture that builds off of failure.
- It's company first, your organization second, and you as a leader third.
- The PowerPoint is dead. Digital CIOs need to communicate with digital products.
- I didn't have a first 100 days. When was the last time you had 100 days to do something?
- Executives who think of IT as free are the least judicious consumers of IT services.
- Digital channels are where people are living their lives. The point of view of the consumer has to be our lens.

- Don't just say that you spend half your time with the business; make sure your calendar reflects that.
- It takes two to be transparent. One who is willing to show and another who is willing to see.
- Having good relationships is the difference between getting support in front of the board or hearing crickets.
- Vision should be something you never attain; you are always just driving toward it.
- The more curious an IT leader, the more effective they will be with the business.
- Shaping IT demand is an investment management practice.
- The key is to market IT's value, not its activity.
- Digital transformation mean shifting ownership of apps, data, and content to the business units.
- If the business has not tried to hire one of my business relationship managers, I am doing something wrong.
- Digital is a marriage between IT and marketing where divorce is not an option.
- IT transformation is more about relationships than technology.
- We don't need a digital strategy—we need a business strategy for a digital world.

Acknowledgments

While in our wedding vows, my husband and I promised that neither of us would have to read each other's books, I am deeply appreciative of his support throughout all of the phases of my career. Most importantly, Tony does not stand for the wine-induced pity parties I tend to throw for myself at the end of a busy week, and reminds me of all of the wonderful things in our lives. Two of those wonderful things are our daughters, Maddy and Audrey, who despite their awe-inspiring sarcasm, are mature, compassionate people in whom I delight every day.

I have this recurring beautiful dream where I come to work and enjoy the company of a dedicated, thoughtful group of colleagues who eat, sleep, and breathe a commitment to Heller Search and our clients. And then I wake up and realize that the dream is a reality. I would like to thank Carol Lynn Thistle, Steve Rovniak, Pam Kurko, Katie Ross, and Lauren O'Connor for their faith in Heller Search and their camaraderie, friendship, counsel, and hard work.

On one auspicious day about fifteen years ago, I had the good fortune to meet Maryfran Johnson, editor-in-chief of *CIO* magazine. From giving me tough editorial critiques, to cautioning me against the purchase of ridiculous shoes, Maryfran has supported me with friendship and guidance ever since.

I delight in my relationship with my friends at CIO.com and the CIO Executive Council. Working with them has been one of the most gratifying professional experiences in my career.

Of course, this book would be but a series of thoughts in my head were it not for the professionalism and attention of my friends at Bibliomotion: Jill Friedlander, Erika Heilman, Jill Schoenhaut, Alicia Simons, and Susan Lauzau.

Finally, I would like to thank, individually, every CIO who over the last decade and a half has given me the generosity of their time and ideas. However, since that list would be a book unto itself, my editor has cautioned me against this idea. Suffice it to say: You know who you are. Thank you.

Notes

I have previously published some of the material in this book in my *Movers and Shakers* blog on CIO.com.

Introduction

1. Eash Sundaram: *The CIO As Champion of Change*, October 6, 2015.
2. John Marcante: *Flywheels, Crowdsourcing, and a New Office of the CTO*, September 30, 2014.
3. John Marcante: *Flywheels, Crowdsourcing, and a New Office of the CTO*, September 30, 2014.
4. Mandy Edwards: *The New IT Operating Model*, September 22, 2015.

Chapter 1

1. Bask Iyer: *Step into the Digital Leadership Void*, September 3, 2015.
2. Dave Truzinksi: *CIO-CDO Dual Role Reinforces the Digital Commitment*, May 20, 2015.
3. Aaron Levie: *The Industrialist's Dilemma*, July 29, 2015.
4. Donagh Herlihy: *The CIO Turned Digital Leader*, August 5, 2015.
5. Andrew Wilson: *CIO TV Is Ready for Prime Time*, May 27, 2015.

Chapter 2

1. Wolfgang Richter: *Dealing with the Accountability vs. Ownership Paradox*, October 13, 2013.

2. Michael Mathias: *Driving Change Through Business Architecture*, November 12, 2013.
3. Jim Fowler: *The CIO Role in the Digital Industrial Economy*, March 29, 2016.
4. Kathy McElligott: *The Business IT Strategy Board*, January 29, 2014.

Chapter 3

1. Bruce Lee: *It Is Time to Deal with the Legacy Below the Surface*, October 29, 2013.
2. Sheryl Bunton: *Mobile Front-End Extends Life of Legacy Systems*, February 25, 2014.
3. John Burke: *Solving the "Big Application" Problem, Amazon Style*, April 29, 2015.

Chapter 4

1. Eric Slavinsky: *The IT Budget Is Also the Company's Budget*, February 16, 2016.
2. Stephen Gold: *Tie Your IT Investments into Revenue*, April 1, 2015.
3. Joe Spagnoletti: *Taking an Investment Management Approach to IT*, January 28, 2015.
4. Jim DuBois: *How Microsoft CIO Jim DuBois Changed the IT operating model*, February 2, 2016.

Chapter 5

1. Scott McKay: *Why CIOs Need to Become "What People" Instead of "How People,"* November 3, 2015.
2. Tim McCabe: *Why Passion Is a Requirement for Today's CIO*, September 29, 2015.
3. Clark Golestani: *The CIO as VC*, September 17, 2014.
4. Kim Stevenson: *How to Develop Your IT High-Potentials*, June 17, 2015.
5. Jim Swanson: *Turning Data into Food*, February 4, 2015.

Chapter 6

1. Malini Balakrishnan: *The Power of Metaphor*, December 17, 2014.
2. Tom Farrah: *The Business Didn't Ask for It*, January 21, 2015.
3. Gerri Martin-Flickinger: *Moving the IT Conversation from Cost to Value*, March 25, 2014.
4. Jay Ferro: *Rebuilding Trust in IT*, July 8, 2015.
5. Michael Smith: *Embrace the Executive Blog*, March 4, 2014.

Chapter 7

1. Jeff Donaldson: *5 Key Qualities IT Leaders Should Cultivate*, November 10, 2015.
2. Dan Olley: *Growing Great Leaders*, February 2, 2014.
3. Kathy Kountze-Tatum: *You've Outsourced the Context. Now What?*, October 22, 2014.
4. Herman De Prins: *Changing the Culture of IT*, January 14, 2015.
5. Marc Franciosa: *Developing Blended Executives*, June 17, 2014.

Chapter 8

1. Rob Lux: *How Freddie Mac Brought Shadow IT into the Light*, February 9, 2016.
2. David Anderson: *The Business Alliance Group*, July 30, 2013.
3. Cora Carmody: *M&A Provides Leadership Opportunities for CIOs*, January 14, 2014.

Chapter 10

1. Steve Zerby: *Building a Culture of Urgency in IT*, May 6, 2015.
2. Bob Logan: *We Are All Plank Owners Now*, July 29, 2014.
3. Brad Strock: *The IT Strategy Behind PayPal's Spinoff from eBay*, January 12, 2016.

Index

About the Author

Martha Heller is president of Heller Search Associates, an executive search firm that specializes in IT leadership positions nationwide across all industries. Her first book, *The CIO Paradox: Battling the Contradictions of IT Leadership* (2012) has become a must-read for IT executives at all levels, and established Heller as one of the most respected voices in the technology industry. Martha has been a contributing writer on CIO.com since 1999, and in 2004 she founded the CIO Executive Council, *CIO* magazine's professional organization for CIOs. As a highly sought after public speaker, Martha has appeared at the National Retail Federation, the Technology Business Management Council, Harvard University, ServiceNow, and Cisco. She is on the selection committee for the CIO 100 awards and the TBM awards. Martha received a B.A. in English from Hamilton College and an M.A. in English from SUNY Stony Brook. She lives in Westborough, Massachusetts with her husband, two daughters, and her beloved little dog.

Follow Martha on twitter (@marthaheller) or visit www.hellersearch.com.